Earth, Inc.

Earth, Inc.

Using Nature's Rules to Build Sustainable Profits

GREGORY UNRUH

Harvard Business Press

Boston, Massachusetts

14 13 12 11 10   5 4 3 2 1

Library of Congress Cataloging-in-Publication Data

Unruh, Gregory.
    Earth, Inc. : using nature's rules to build sustainable profits / Gregory Unruh.
        p. cm.
    ISBN 978-1-4221-2717-9 (hbk. : alk. paper)   1. New products—
Environmental aspects.   2. Industrial management—Environmental aspects.
3. Production management—Environmental aspects.   I. Title.
    TS170.5.U55 2010
    658.4'083—dc22

                                                                2009010177

The paper used in this publication meets the requirements of the American
National Standard for Permanence of Paper for Publications and Documents
in Libraries and Archives Z39.48-1992.

The text of this book is printed using soy-based ink. The paper used for the
jacket contains 10 percent post consumer waste, and the paper used for the
text contains 30 percent post consumer waste. Both are certified by the Forest
Stewardship Council (FSC), an independent, non-governmental, not-for-profit
organization established to promote the responsible management of the world's
forests.

Mixed Sources
Product group from well-managed
forests, controlled sources and
recycled wood or fiber
www.fsc.org   Cert no. SGS-COC-005368
© 1996 Forest Stewardship Council

FSC

Contents

Acknowledgments

Like all books, this one is a group effort that started at home with the support of my wife and family. It would also have been impossible without the editorial guidance of the professionals at Harvard Business Press, including Jacqueline Murphy, Kathleen Carr, Bronwyn Fryer, Karen Dillon, and Hollis Heimbouch, as well as Sona Partners' Timothy Ogden and Laura Starita. I also appreciate the support of my colleagues at Thunderbird School of Global Management, especially Thunderbird President Angel Cabrera. In addition, the book has benefited from the generous time and mentoring of a long list of people including Dr. Sultan Ahmed Al Jaber, Khaled Awad, John Beck, Steven Bishop, Jay Bolus, Steve Bradfield, John Bradford, Michael Braungart, Sumi Cate, Scott Charon, Todd Copeland, Jill Dumain, James Ewell, Gerry Fishbeck, Miguel Fluxà, Dan Godamunne, James Hagan, Ted Howes, Santiago Iniguez, Lindsay James, Scott Johnson, Marwan Khaisheh, William McDonough, William Moomaw, Bill Morrissey, Eric Nelson, Sarah Cordero Pinchansky, Michael Realff, Carlos Sanchez, Rudy Vetter, Scott Vitters, and Gabe Wing, among others. Finally, I want to acknowledge my mother and father, who, while not living to see the publication of this book, supported me throughout the years prior to its writing.

Introduction

Look deep into nature, and then you will
understand everything better.
—Albert Einstein

"Business sustainability? Embed it and forget it." As soon as I said it, the journalist furrowed his brow. I knew the inevitable follow-up was coming. "Embed sustainability and forget it? How can you say that? Sustainability is a huge problem for business managers. You can't just tell them to solve it and forget it." Yes, you can. And that's what this book is about.

Most executives have come to frame sustainability as a "journey," a potentially endless expedition of incremental improvement. In my 2008 *Harvard Business Review* article, I argued that while achieving sustainability requires time and often incremental improvement, sustainability is a known destination.[1] We know exactly what sustainability looks like because we interact with a sustainable production system every day. And the system is time and battle tested; it's been running continuously for millennia. Refined through billions of years of trial and error, our sustainability model is the Earth's biosphere. We'll reach the sustainability destination when we embed the principles that account for the biosphere's sustainability to business practice in profitable ways. Embed it and forget it.

If you have picked up this book, you are probably already sold on the larger "business case for sustainability." You most likely know that the benefits of greening and greater social responsibility have been largely demonstrated in theory and practice. (See Further Reading for previous publications that develop the larger business case for sustainability and its benefits.) I am not going to rehash the basic evidence that has been covered elsewhere (although a crib sheet is offered in table I-1 that managers can use to think through the potential gains). Granted, none of the observed benefits of greening are automatic. Like all good strategies, success depends on competent execution and rapid learning from missteps. However, when done right, sustainability pays. Likewise, when neglected, sustainability can cost you. Just ask Royal Dutch Shell managers who were famously blindsided by the twin Brent Spar and Nigerian crises in 1995. Or General Electric's decades-long entanglement over asbestos and PCB-related cleanups. Or Mattel managers who faced a 2007 firestorm for selling toys coated with poisonous lead paint. Or the hundreds of retailers furiously yanking products containing bisphenol A from their shelves in 2008. Or Florida home-builders pressured to remove corrosive drywall from customer's homes in 2009. Undoubtedly, many companies have similar sustainability time bombs waiting for the prying eyes of activists or the press to set them off.

While answering the big question of the "business case" is absolutely necessary for managers to gain buy-in and budget to launch sustainability initiatives, it is insufficient. I'm not writing this book to create another "me too" argument for the big-picture benefits of sustainability. I'm writing because the question I now hear most often from managers trying to implement sustainability initiatives is not, "Why should we be sustainable?" but "So what do we do?"

This is a "how-to" book of environmental sustainability. That is, how companies can align their operations, products, and processes with ecology in a lasting way that not only resolves environmental conflicts, but creates value for the enterprise. Profitability is a key part of sustainability. Business initiatives that fail to deliver profit—that is, create value in excess of costs— are unsustainable, regardless of how ecofriendly they are. Luckily for profit-seeking managers, the biosphere is a value-creating, value-multiplying, and value-accumulating machine, which bodes well for companies seeking to tap into its secrets.

Where the Biosphere and Industry Diverge

The best way to understand the difference between the biosphere and industry is to look at the model managers use to strategize about production: the *value chain* (see figure I-1). The value chain

FIGURE I-1

The value chain

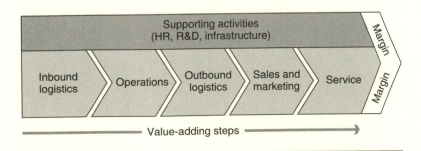

Supporting activities (HR, R&D, infrastructure)

Inbound logistics | Operations | Outbound logistics | Sales and marketing | Service

Margin

Value-adding steps

represents the manufacturing steps that take a low-value raw material like iron ore and turn it into a high-value product, like a Mercedes-Benz S-Class luxury sedan. It's been called the "value chain" ever since Harvard professor Michael Porter coined the term in his 1985 bestseller *Competitive Advantage*. In Porter's world, the chain hopefully ends with a satisfied customer.[2] What Porter's model leaves out, unfortunately, is what happens when the value chain interacts with the biosphere.

The environmental scientist's equivalent to the value chain is called a Linear Type 1 ecology, colloquially known as a "take-make-waste" system. As figure I-2 shows, this model takes into account the value chain's interactions with the natural world. The production process takes resources from the environment, makes them into products but also creates waste—including the product itself at the end of its life—and sends all this waste to the landfill. To demonstrate the inefficiency of this system, Insead Business School professor Robert Ayres once calculated that over 95 percent of all resources extracted from the environment become waste within six months from harvest.[3] The pharmaceutical industry is a good example: a ton of salable pills requires well over 150 tons of raw

FIGURE I-2

The value chain in its biospheric context

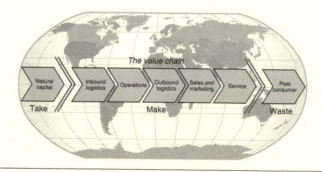

materials.[4] The energy industry profile is similar. Coal-fired electric power stations waste two-thirds of their input energy before the first electron zips out of the plant.

I encountered the environmental consequences of the value chain as an environmental consultant in the1980s, remediating the toxic waste problems of companies like Shell, Chevron, Hewlett-Packard, and Apple. I started my job with typical post-college enthusiasm, expecting that my work would change the way businesses did theirs. After the first few projects, however, it became clear that my job more resembled that of a housekeeper than a revolutionary. Though we used the technical term *remediation*, I was really there to clean up messes, like chasing down toxic chemicals that had escaped from a company's containment lagoon.

After a year or two of remediation work, I realized I was working at the wrong end of the value chain. I began arguing to my bosses that we should get out of remediation and into the business of *pre*mediation, which is preventing the spills in the first place by redesigning the products, process, and behaviors that caused them. Instead, when I argued to an operations manager at a chemical plant that he should premediate his facility by doing away with toxic chemicals, he said, "Changing the process isn't worth it. We're just going to install a filter on the end of the waste line and pull all the toxic stuff into a leakproof containment system." He seemed to be oblivious to the fact that we were there dealing with the aftermath of the last "leakproof" system.

Frustrated, I went back to graduate school in search of a better answer. What I discovered was the emerging discipline of *industrial ecology*, an approach that envisioned industry as ecosystems of interdependent facilities, trading wastes in sustainable ways. The more recent development of *biomimicry* is a sophisticated offshoot of industrial ecology thinking. Among the many tools developed by industrial ecologists, one was especially good at clarifying the environmental problems with value chain thinking: *life cycle assessment*. Known to practitioners as the "LCA," life cycle assessment measures a product's environmental impacts through the entire value chain, from cradle to grave.

LCAs were done on a range of products, from cars to diapers, and proved excellent at pointing out where the environmental insults were. Most companies then went after the identified problems using a strategy of *eco-efficiency*, popularized by the Switzerland-based World Business Council for Sustainable Development (WBCSD). Eco-efficiency puts the value chain on a diet, with the goal of producing more outputs with less waste. Because eco-efficiency could produce an environmental and economic win-win, many companies rightfully welcomed it. It was obviously not the end game, however. Eco-efficiency just slows the extraction of resources and production of wastes; it doesn't eliminate them. It's the equivalent of cutting back from two packs of cigarettes a day to one. Industrial ecologists recognized this but had a hard time convincing business and governmental decision makers to adopt the more radical vision of eliminating waste.

At this point, I was fortunate to meet William McDonough, an architect and designer who had helped a number of companies implement what he and his partner Michael Braungart called the "cradle-to-cradle" protocol. Like industrial ecology thinking, the fundamental principle of cradle-to-cradle is that in nature one creature's waste is another's food. By building closed-loop systems, companies could entirely eliminate what we think of as waste. McDonough's clients had been convinced to apply his ideas mostly because he is a very convincing guy. I wanted to know if such efforts would be profitable, in other words, if they would survive and thrive in the marketplace without McDonough's considerable charisma. So he and I cofounded the Center for Eco-Intelligent Management at the IE Business School in Spain to better understand the business case for sustainability initiatives.

As I studied different companies that were implementing varieties of sustainability initiatives, common threads began to emerge. But these threads were not just shared by businesses that were profiting from sustainability. They were remarkably similar to the principles that make the biosphere sustainable. The biosphere, like a corporation, is a profit-making venture. Value in nature continuously accumulates through innovation. But in order to be sustainable on the finite planet Earth, innovation is paradoxically constrained.

When I tell managers and experts this, they inevitably recoil. "Constrain innovation?" they say. "But everyone knows that business growth depends on innovation!" While I agree, and I am not talking about constraining growth, the managers' reaction comes from a widely shared misconception. The response is a gut reaction from the legacy of the environmental debate and the "limits to growth" discourse that has roots in the ideas of the eighteenth-century economist Thomas Malthus. Malthusians argue that the Earth's carrying capacity is limited, and to ensure we don't overshoot the limits, humans need to limit or constrain economic growth. This antigrowth agenda is obviously an anathema to most executives when shareholders demand increases in sales and earnings each quarter.

While innovation in the biosphere *is* constrained in very special ways, the growth and wealth of the biosphere have not suffered. With millions of different species, it's clear that the restrictions do not limit the profuse creativity of nature. These constraints have not prevented the creation of a vast number of technological innovations that humble our best scientists and engineers. The biosphere's constraints do not exist to limit growth. They serve to ensure that short-term growth doesn't threaten the long-term health of the planet. Likewise, by implementing the appropriate constraints, innovative business growth should also be able to continue without jeopardizing the planet's future.

In examining the biosphere, what becomes immediately obvious is that there is no linear value chain extracting resources and spewing out wastes. Instead there is a *value cycle* (see figure I-3). Within nature's value cycle, a select number of raw materials are constantly reused—and never lose value. They are literally rein-

FIGURE I-3

An industrial adaptation of nature's value cycle

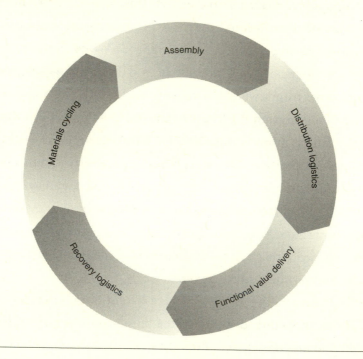

carnated cyclically into new beings. Nature's material assets are churned over and over in a process of never-ending propagation. And the system never stands still. It is constantly innovating and evolving to become more complex, specialized, and effective. Managers who hope to improve productivity and bolster growth can certainly learn a few things from nature.

Creating a value cycle is at the core of business sustainability strategy. But companies cannot build a value cycle by merely taking their existing value chain and bending it back on itself. Doing so will only create a costly mess. To be economically viable, a series of methodical, enabling steps have to be taken first. Like premediation, these steps can be considered "precycling." Before a profitable value cycle can start churning, the conditions for success have to be put in place. Precycling is therefore something that occurs first in the heads of new product designers, operations managers, and strategic executives. Precycling is a managerial mind-set that replaces the value chain model with value cycle thinking.

Taken together, I call the precycling steps the biosphere rules. They serve as a framework to help managers figure out the specific actions they can take to make their products and their organizations more sustainable. Of course, every business is different, and so no one can create a one-size-fits-all sustainability to-do list. Although the steps are not strictly linear, most organizations will be more successful by following them in order through a single product or through the entire company. In later chapters, we'll look at a few examples of massive initiatives that failed because the companies took the steps out of order. What the biosphere rules provide is a systematic approach to thinking about sustainability in your organization, allowing you to create a customized and practical to-do list for your company.

The Biosphere Rules

The biosphere rules are five deep-seated principles inspired by the value cycle operations of the biosphere. These principles were perfected over three-and-a-half billion years ago and encoded into every living thing on the planet long before humans existed, much less created such things as writing, agriculture, commerce, modern industry, and the information revolution. These five principles or rules are:

1 *Materials parsimony.* Minimize the types of materials used in products with a focus on materials that are life-friendly and economically recyclable.
2 *Power autonomy.* Maximize the power autonomy of products and processes so they can function on renewable energy.
3 *Value cycles.* Recover and reincarnate materials from end-of-use goods into new value-added products.
4 *Sustainable product platforms.* Leverage your value cycle as a product platform for profitable scale, scope, and knowledge economies.
5 *Function over form.* Fulfill customers' functional needs in ways that sustain the value cycle.

The rules are simple, but interpreting and integrating them into a company's business model take care and attention. And of course, the biosphere and business are not exact analogues, so the rules also require adaptation to an individual business's context and situation. Again, they provide a framework for identifying not why to do sustainability, but what to do and in what order, to reach the destination of sustainability.

Each of the rules serves as the basis for the chapters that follow, where we'll look at how the rule works in nature, how the business world works today, strategies for change, case studies of leaders, and how to confront implementation challenges.

Easing Implementation

Sustainability innovation is obviously a big challenge for most companies. It is a long-term effort requiring long-term strategic investment. These realities will quickly run up against the short-term managerial demands to produce financial results on a quarterly basis. Furthermore, the near-term costs of change are far more tangible and easy to quantify than the contingent far-off benefits. I rephrase the title of a *Harvard Business Review* article by Harvard professor Robert Kaplan, "Must sustainability investment be justified by faith alone?" Following Kaplan's logic, the tangible and intangible business benefits may be difficult to quantify, but they are not zero (see table I-1). And when conservative managers assign a value of zero, they are choosing to be "precisely wrong" rather than "vaguely right."[5] In the end, management will have to make a determination on the value and need for such sustainability investments. That requires complex judgment on what the future holds that cannot be reduced to a simple "business case." In recognition of the uncertainty, the biosphere rules presented here are designed to be implemented in sequence in order to minimize initial investment, reduce initial risks, and lower the organizational barriers to change.

In some companies, trying to implement the biosphere rules in one fell swoop is a recipe for violent backlash. For this reason, the rules are organized as steps, each producing its own near-term

TABLE I-1

The business benefits of implementing the biosphere rules

Biosphere rule	Business benefit
Materials parsimony	Reduced supplier complexity
	Reduced production complexity
	Reduced toxics risk
	Reduced compliance costs
	Volume purchase discounts
	Improved health and safety
	Improved worker productivity
	Improved product attributes
	Improved environmental performance
Power autonomy	Reduced energy costs
	Reduced compliance costs
	Reduced processing costs
	Improved environmental performance
	Improved customer performance
	Optimized for renewable energy
Value cycles	Input cost savings
	Reduced processing costs
	Reduced supplier risk
	Increased control over brand and reputation
	Improved asset management
	Improved customer information
Sustainable product platforms	Compound above benefits through scale
	Compound above benefits through scope
	Foundation to accumulate learning by doing
	Build robust cross-industry platform demand

TABLE I-1 (*continued*)

Function over form	Generate ongoing revenue stream
	Greater customer knowledge
	Increase control over asset base
	Convergence into expanded offerings

win. But while the biosphere rules are broken into largely self-contained steps, it must be remembered that they work together as parts of an integrated sustainable business system. This requires that managers conceive of their business as a larger system, a system that incorporates not just their own operations, but also their suppliers and customers. This extended view of the company is an important shift in managerial mindset. But by implementing all of the biosphere rules, companies can reach a state of *embedded sustainability* where sustainable practice is internalized into a company's products and processes and vanishes as a managerial concern. Managers often view this as a far-reaching, futuristic goal, but they are wrong. Embedded sustainability is completely achievable with current technology and today's know-how. Anyone who doubts it need only go outside and be awed by the productivity of nature. A snail doesn't wake up and ask, "How will I be sustainable today?" When the biosphere rules are successfully implemented, managers won't have to either.

In the chapters that follow, we'll look at each of the biosphere rules in terms of business need and business benefit, examine cases of companies that are already profitably implementing the rule (and occasionally peek at initiatives that failed so mistakes can be avoided), and look at practical steps for implementing the rule. You might note that among many stories of cutting-edge innovations I've included some examples that might seem somewhat dated—steps some companies took more than a decade ago. I've chosen these stories purposefully because many managers tell me they are worried about being on the "bleeding edge," trying to get corporate buy-in for untested initiatives. As you'll see from these examples, building in sustainability isn't bleeding edge anymore. These stories also show that profiting from building in sustainability is sustainable. The successes you'll read about are not the result of fads or a temporary change in the business context. Many companies have been profiting from sustainability for years and continue to do so.

As you finish each chapter, you should already have some ideas for steps that are appropriate for your company and your situation. By the end of the book, I hope you'll agree that sustainability is a destination, not a journey, and that you now have a road map for how to get there. It won't be easy, but if we know anything about the current state of the world, it's that standing still is no longer an option.

1

Materials Parsimony

RULE 1

Minimize the types of materials used in products with
a focus on materials that are life-friendly and
economically recyclable.

---

*Entia non sunt multiplicanda praeter necessitate. (Entities
should not be multiplied without necessity.)*
—William of Ockham (ca. 1285–1349)

In January 2008, if you had walked into any sporting goods
retailer, particularly one focused on the outdoors such as East-
ern Mountain Sports or REI, you would have found a large dis-
play of water bottles and cooking implements made from a
wonder plastic invented more than forty years ago called polycarbonate. Most carried the Nalgene brand. Polycarbonate bottles

and the like were wildly popular among the outdoors and sporting set because they are lightweight and nearly unbreakable. You can accidentally drop the bottle off the edge of a cliff and be confident that once you get to the bottom to retrieve it, it will still be intact.

If you walked into the same store in August 2008, you would have found no polycarbonate water bottles. Why? Because one of the two major ingredients of polycarbonate is bisphenol A (BPA), a chemical at the center of a furious debate about possible negative health effects. As I'm writing, the debate over BPA still rages. The key questions are what levels of exposure to BPA are unsafe and how likely is a person to be exposed to unsafe levels of BPA through the plastics the chemical is used to make. Where the science is soundest is in BPA's effects on the endocrine system in infants—the vast majority of the attention has been focused on the use of BPA in baby bottles—because exposure to BPA increases when plastics containing the chemical are heated (as baby bottles often are), and because of infants' small size and rapid development, smaller concentrations of any chemical can have an outsized effect. While this may seem sufficient reason to pull polycarbonate water bottles from stores, keep in mind that the science isn't settled. BPA has not, as of this writing, been declared toxic by any government agency.

Still, Nalgene, a company whose name has become as synonymous with polycarbonate water bottles as Kleenex is to, well, Kleenex, has had to shift its product line to entirely new materials in months. Retailers around the world preemptively pulled polycarbonate products from their shelves. Consumers, retailers, and Nalgene itself simply decided that this wonder plastic was not worth using. It's still too soon to estimate total costs from what is essentially a consumer-behavior–driven recall, but it must be in the hundreds of millions of dollars. And these costs are not being borne by the companies that invented BPA and polycarbonate plastic. For now at least, the responsibility is squarely in the lap of companies that used and sold products made from the material. It's a scenario that has been repeated with increasing frequency over the past decade and shows no sign of abating.

Materials chemistry has created innumerable wonders, from metal alloys to plastic polymers, but the proliferation has become too much of a good thing. With over one hundred thousand different synthetic chemicals (no one really seems to know the exact number), management of material complexity and risks has become a real chore. Standards and regulations have not been much help. Since 1979, the U.S. Environmental Protection Agency (EPA) has imposed restrictions on only 9 of the 32,559 new chemical applications it has received (and certainly didn't issue any restrictions on the use of BPA or polycarbonate plastics). While a boon for chemical manufacturers, this situation has put their customers at risk. Thanks to a U.S. legal rule called "joint and several liability," anyone in the value chain who handles materials that are discovered to be hazardous can be held responsible for the entire cleanup.[1]

Dow Chemical has recently found that a company can be held responsible even if it's not connected to an incident. One of the most internationally infamous industrial accidents is the 1984 release of toxic gas by a Union Carbide plant in Bhopal, India. The accident ultimately led to the deaths of twenty thousand people; the plant and the surrounding area are still contaminated. In 2001, Dow Chemical bought some of the assets of Union Carbide, but not the division, which had been sold to another company years before, that had operated the Bhopal plant. However, in August 2008, Indian government officials stated that they will vigorously pursue Dow for civil and criminal liabilities related to the Bhopal disaster.[2] In 2009, more than a dozen U.S. lawmakers signed a letter asking Dow to take responsibility for clean up of the site.[3] Even if Dow is released from this liability, the confusion is disconcerting and potentially costly for Dow shareholders.[4]

Given the dearth of government oversight, the public has been holding brand owners responsible for what goes into their products, and many companies are responding to these new expectations. As businesses take on this responsibility, most quickly recognize they have only a limited understanding of the materials—and risks—they are putting into their products.

In contrast, nature has none of these problems, thanks largely to the principle of materials parsimony. For business, materials parsimony, the first biosphere rule, can reduce risk, complexity, and costs (see table 1-1), certainly a winning busi-

TABLE 1-1

The business benefits of materials parsimony

Biosphere rule	Business benefit
Materials parsimony	Reduced supplier complexity
	Reduced production complexity
	Reduced toxics risk
	Reduced compliance costs
	Volume purchase discounts
	Improved health and safety
	Improved worker productivity
	Improved product attributes
	Improved environmental performance

ness proposition. But more important, it sets the foundations for subsequent biosphere rules that allow companies to economically close production loops. This chapter will introduce the tools that companies are adopting to manage toxic materials risk and create a sustainable materials palette for building products and, ultimately, value cycles.

Nature's Way

Aristotle was a great student of nature, and during his long life, he sought to categorize all living things. His observations led him to conclude that "the more perfect a nature is, the fewer means it requires for its operation." His idea was picked up in the fourteenth century by the medieval logician William of Ockham, who crafted it into the law of parsimony.[5] Translated from the Latin, the law says, "Entities should not be multiplied without necessity." Two hundred years later, Renaissance man Leonardo da Vinci reinterpreted the saying as, "Simplicity is the ultimate sophistication." Today we simply say, "Less is more."

The law of parsimony is manifest in the material choices made by nature long ago, which allow the diversity present in the biosphere today. No one can deny the sophistication of nature's production. The biosphere creates hard materials, such as bone, shells, and teeth, as well as soft materials, such as eyeballs, slime, and silk. It creates on all scales, from the microscopic diatom to the city-sized coral reef. Yet nature manufactures all its products using an incredibly small number of fundamental and, by necessity, nontoxic materials. This materials parsimony is the biosphere's first rule and the sustainability principle that underlies everything in it.

Every teenager in secondary school learns the periodic table of the elements—the universe's material palette encompassing the 88 naturally occurring elements from arsenic to xenon. Yet from ninety or so naturally occurring options, nature uses just four elements—carbon, hydrogen, oxygen, and nitrogen—as the basis for every living thing on earth. Adding small amounts of sulfur and phosphorous, and some other elements for specialty purposes like calcium used in bones, this sparse palette can account for 99 percent of the weight of every living thing on the planet (see table 1-2). For the most part, it is carbon, hydrogen, oxygen, and nitrogen, known to organic chemists as "CHON," which compose the bulk of nature's productivity. Nature uses the CHON elements to form amino acids, proteins, and sugars that in turn are used to build cells and then organs like the kidneys or the brain. But atoms from those same elements could just as easily end up as a single-celled bacterium or the petal of an orchid.

The parsimony inherent in nature's materials palette has not resulted in a commensurate parsimony of creativity. It is not,

TABLE 1-2

Materials parsimony in the biosphere

Element	Symbol	Percentage
Oxygen	O	62%
Carbon	C	20%
Hydrogen	H	10%
Nitrogen	N	3%
Calcium	Ca	2.5%
Phosphorus	P	1.14%
Sulfur, potassium, sodium, magnesium, iodine, iron, chlorine	S, K, Na, Mg, I, Fe, Cl	Trace amounts

therefore, the materials that determine the diversity seen in nature, but the various forms and functions into which those materials are molded.

Rule 1: Materials Parsimony

The materials parsimony rule guides a rethinking of input sourcing decisions and a dramatic simplification of the number and types of materials used in products. Materials parsimony should not be confused with the environmental management strategy of *eco-efficiency*. Eco-efficiency is about the *quantity* of materials being used in products. Materials parsimony is instead about the number of *types* of materials used, regardless of quantity.

Asking business to copy nature and use the same four inputs takes things a bit too far. Our production technologies are not yet sophisticated enough to emulate nature's manufacturing methods. Most businesses still have needs for specific specialty materials for key functions. But companies can nonetheless look to nature to understand the benefits of simplifying their materials palette. Many could dramatically reduce the number of materials employed, mimicking nature with a small number of materials doing the yeoman's work, and reserving a smaller set of materials for special isolated applications. This is just like nature's use of trace elements.

One look at our modern industrial landscape and it quickly becomes clear that materials parsimony has not been business's guiding principle. Our economy is filled with an ever-growing diversity of materials from organic fibers to synthetic plastics. Industry's materials innovation has clearly been a boon to business and to many consumers. Plastics alone have created whole new product markets from "rubber" duckies to artificial hearts. But this broad proliferation of materials is not cost free. And sustainability concerns are now forcing companies to confront the downside of modern materials proliferation.

Thus far, corporate pioneers that have begun simplifying their input materials have been motivated predominantly by risk management concerns. Driven by potential toxic liabilities and a growing corporate ethic of total product responsibility, a select number of companies have begun using management tools to evaluate the health and environmental implications of their material sourcing choices. This is a good first step and in accord with the biosphere: nature's palette is not just parsimonious but also largely nontoxic. But there is another reason for pursuing parsimony that most managers have yet to recognize: a parsimonious materials palette is a vital first step for cost-effective recycling. In nature, the building blocks of the biosphere, the CHON elements, are always at hand for easy reuse, no sorting or long distance transport required. In fact, CHON elements are among the most abundant in the universe. For business, selecting a parsimonious palette consisting of nontoxic and reusable materials not only carries inherent benefits but is also a key foundational step for the other biosphere rules.

Unwanted Surprises

Historians divide human history in material ages, from stone to iron. And we have long equated this succession of ages with human progress. One or two millennia from now when archeologists are digging in the layers corresponding to the twentieth and twenty-first centuries, they will likely encounter a stratum of synthetic materials several inches wide (and much thicker than that in our landfills!). The lucky archeologist who finds it will cry out to his colleagues across the dig, "Hey, I've found the plastic people!"

Our modern plastic age seriously took off in the 1960s, epitomized by DuPont's well-known motto, "Better things for better living through chemistry." In the more than four decades since then, thousands of synthetic chemicals, plastics, and other materials have been produced and sold on the open market. It is estimated that material manufacturers add one thousand new chemicals to their product lines each year. And there is no end to the proliferation in sight.

It's much easier to create a new compound than to assess its human or environmental impacts. Evaluating toxicity requires costly and time-consuming testing. Manufacturers have thus avoided such testing, and to date, only a fraction of the synthetic chemicals available on the marketplace have undergone detailed human or environmental health risk assessments.[6] This dearth of information means we usually don't know for certain if a synthetic material is toxic or at what concentration any toxicity might pose a danger to humans and the environment, let alone how it reacts with other chemicals. Our lack of understanding has meant inevitable unwanted surprises.

For example, when Steve Jobs and Steve Wozniak released their first personal computer on April Fool's Day in 1976, it looked as if a clean new industry was born. The joke, however, seems to have been on us. Not long after the birth of Apple, cracks began to appear in the industry's clean façade. In 1981, Silicon Valley resident Lorraine Ross gave birth to a daughter with a rare heart defect. By canvassing the neighborhood, she found she was not alone. Miscarriages, cancers, and birth disorders in parts of Silicon Valley proved to be three times higher than normal. The culprits were the underground chemical storage tanks that every high-tech campus in Silicon Valley used. Most had leaked, leaving Silicon Valley with the highest concentration of Superfund sites in the United States today.[7]

My first job as a professional environmental consultant was to track down pollutants and remediate the groundwater contamination in Silicon Valley. Despite the "clean room" impression, electronics production requires some nastily toxic substances. These include chlorinated and brominated substances, heavy metals, and acids. What I soon discovered was that once these pollutants are released into the environment, cleaning them up is a practical impossibility. Trying to get toxic waste out of contaminated soil or water is like trying to put toothpaste back into a tube—you can never shove it all back in. And because many chemicals are hazardous at very low concentrations, a small amount is a big problem. The cost of trying to remediate a contaminated site was huge. In one typical case, my clients spent well over $10 million just trying to figure out how extensive the problem was. Then it cost many times that to develop a strategy for controlling the pollution and preventing it from spreading further.

On a national scale the U.S. Congressional Budget Office estimates that the cost of Superfund, the regulatory regime created in 1980 to clean up contaminated industrial sites, will be $230 billion through 2070—70 percent of this cost is incurred by the polluters.[8] Other estimates put the private sector cost at almost $450 billion, ten times the annual revenues of the chemical industry itself.[9] But while getting toxins like these out of groundwater and soil has been a major headache, a whole new set of toxic materials issues are arising that may make our remediation work in the 1980s look like child's play.

In 1997, 3M made a surprising discovery during a routine check of factory workers' blood.[10] As expected, the blood of all the 3M employees had small quantities of the chemical perfluo-rooctane sulfonate (PFOS)—a key input used in the production of 3M's renowned stain-resistant spray Scotchgard. The problem was with the control samples taken from nonemployees. Since the people in the control group had never been in the plant or exposed to the production process, their blood should have been "clean." It wasn't. Detectable concentrations of PFOS turned up in all of them. Hoping there was some mistake, 3M's medical director got samples from six hundred Red Cross donors and tested them. There was PFOS in all of these samples too. He then obtained samples from Europe, comfortably far away from the 3M facility. They all tested positive. It seemed that everyone in the world was contaminated with 3M's product. And not just people. Polar bears in the Arctic, birds in Japan—just about everywhere anyone looked they found 3M's PFOS.

Regulators like the U.S. Environmental Protection Agency were just as surprised as 3M to discover that everyone in the world had been contaminated with the synthetic chemical and have only now begun studying the potential implications. PFOS is part of the larger perfluorochemical (PFC) family that includes sister chemicals like PFOA, a key ingredient in Teflon. In fact, PFCs are found in a wide variety of products including furniture, clothing, cosmetics, medical applications, and food packaging. And while PFCs have not been conclusively shown to be toxic or hazardous, their properties of persistence and bio-accumulation that account for their ubiquity in living things are concerning. In May 2000, 3M voluntarily shut down its PFOS plant, a business that had been profitable for over fifty years.[11] In 2006, the EPA asked companies to voluntarily eliminate the use of PFOA in products by 2015.

Voluntary actions aside, PFC concerns are already causing losses for companies. In 2004, for example, panic ensued in

China when the public got wind that the U.S. EPA had alleged that DuPont failed to disclose the potential PFOA risks of its Teflon products. Boycotts ensued and major Chinese department stores began pulling Teflon-coated pans from the shelves. The public response has so far been more muted in the United States, but consumer advocate groups have begun recommending that customers go back to good old cast-iron cookware.

Scotchgard and Teflon may be the tip of the iceberg, however. Since 3M's discovery, scientists have found the issue goes far beyond individual compounds like PFOS and PFOA. Public health surveys show that the average person harbors over one hundred forty industrial chemicals in his or her body, all of which were invented in the past seventy-five years.[12] This situation is now ominously described by experts as "body burden." The most troubling chemicals, such as PCBs, dioxin, and PFCs, are persistent and bio-accumulate. Many also bio-magnify so that what starts out as minute contamination in microscopic sea plankton, measured in parts per million, becomes intensified thousands of times through the food chain. At the top of the food chain is human breast milk, where the highest concentrations of industrial chemicals are found.

Who Is Responsible?

If, as has happened in the past, important health or environmental hazards are found to be associated with body burden the risk to companies could be astronomical. How are you going to remediate a chemical problem that lies in the tissue of every living mammal on the planet? And once toxic contamination is discovered, it doesn't take long for people to start pointing fingers. 3M apparently found no solace in the uncertainty over the impact of certain chemical substances like PFOS on humans and took the dramatic step of shutting down its business.

The situation today is clear: companies may be held responsible by governments and consumers for every material and component that goes into their products. Ignorance is no longer a defense; neither is trying to pass the responsibility off to suppliers. Proactive companies are acting on this understanding. As one product manager told me, "It's just no longer acceptable to us to use materials without understanding their full impacts. We want to know what's going into our products."[13] To respond to this reality, new management tools have emerged.

Green Screens: A First Step Toward Materials Parsimony

With toxic responsibility, the buck stops at the finished product brand. It is the brand, after all, that customers—whether business-to-business or business-to-consumer—associate most fully with the product. But given the incredible diversity of chemicals and products available, many managers may find it difficult to figure out exactly which suppliers, much less which chemicals and synthetics, are part of their extended supply chain. Over the past decade, a new sustainability management tool has emerged to make this easier for managers: *green screens*. Green screens provide a process for systematically scrutinizing input sourcing decisions to weed out potential toxins and hazards from a company's supply chain. Green screens range from the simple, like lists of prohibited chemicals, to the sophisticated, like protocols requiring extensive laboratory testing.

A good example of a simple green screen is one used by the Swedish apparel manufacturer and retailer Hennes & Mauritz,

Inc. (H&M). H&M is a major user of cotton and synthetic fibers, including polyester and nylon, as well as a variety of chemical dyes. In 1993, German legislation banned some types of Azo dyes, a chemical commonly used in the textile industry to color fabrics. The regulatory action led H&M to consider more deeply the toxic implications of its sourcing decisions. While chemical suppliers worked on the assumption that materials were safe until proven toxic, H&M decided to take a different tack. The company adopted the "precautionary principle" to guide its sourcing decisions. The precautionary principle says that indication of risk, not proof of risk, is all that is needed to sideline a material. To implement its new approach, H&M in effect created its own chemical regulations for operations worldwide. It began with the Azo dyes banned in Germany and prohibited them in all its products, everywhere. It then sought out other suspect chemicals and added them to the list. H&M then required suppliers to ensure that their products be free of the chemicals on the list. The company now updates its list every two or three years, adding new substances or lowering the allowable limits of already listed chemicals.[14] H&M's list currently has over one hundred seventy prohibited compounds.

At the other end of the spectrum from H&M's simple, restricted chemical list are protocols that go well beyond bans based on existing information. These protocols often rely on independent laboratory testing of chemicals to determine if there are potential human health and environmental risks. One of the first protocols was devised by the Environmental Protection Encouragement Agency (EPEA), a consultancy founded in Germany by Michael Braungart in 1987. Braungart, a chemist by training, is one of the organizers of Greenpeace Germany's chemical program. Based on his Greenpeace experiences, Braungart established EPEA to help companies pursue a greener path.

One of EPEA's key innovations was a methodology for assessing chemicals, creating one of the first sophisticated green screens.[15]

Today the screening methodology, known as the MBDC (McDonough Braungart Design Consultants) Protocol, examines the makeup of a client's product down to the molecular level. This can be a daunting task. A seemingly simple product like a desk chair can have over six hundred individual chemicals to be evaluated.[16] The results of the chemical analysis place each of the component materials into one of four categories: green, yellow, orange, or red. Green materials are those that pose little or no risk and can be used without concern for environmental or health threats. Yellow chemicals pose a moderate risk but are considered acceptable for use until a green alternative can be identified. Orange means that there are no indications of high risk, but that not enough information is available to ensure safety. This category is essentially flagged until more data is collected. A red rating means that there is high risk and that the material should be phased out as soon as is feasible. Red chemicals are mostly confirmed carcinogens, endocrine disruptors, mutagens, reproductive toxins, and teratogens (agents that cause birth defects or other malformations). The protocol, in effect, does the work of a governmental regulator determining which materials are hazardous and which are acceptable.

Green-Screen Challenges: Managing the Unknown

While a useful management tool, all green-screening efforts are dependent on one important resource: *information*. Putative green screeners quickly find that it is a resource in short supply. Disclosure of information about chemical risks and hazards has a patchy history. The earliest examples go back over four thousand years to Egyptian physicians scribbling medicine warnings for their patients on papyrus. Things haven't changed much since then. Today the state-of-the-art chemical management tool is the material safety data sheet, or MSDS, created in 1983 by the U.S. Occupational Safety and Health Administration (OSHA). However, the MSDS contains relatively little information of use to managers who are trying to green screen.

When True Textiles, a fabric manufacturer, began its first green-screening effort in 1995, it turned to MSDSs. It found them woefully unsuited to the task. As its provenance indicates, the MSDS is mostly focused on how to handle the material in its pure form and how to clean up a spill. In general, the MSDS doesn't provide detailed information about the ingredients used to make the material or how the material interacts with other compounds. True Textiles quickly recognized it was going to have to go to its suppliers for greater detail about product chemistry.

You might think it would be easy to ask suppliers for chemical information, but it's not, for a couple of reasons. First, the disaggregated nature of the chemical industry results in a number of blind spots. When True Textiles approached its suppliers about material chemistry, it found that many were just as uninformed about the deep chemistry of their products as True Textiles was. The reason is multitiered chemical supply chains: a single material can be made with multiple inputs from multiple contractors. Because information is fragmented along a complex chain, some suppliers know precious little about the chemical composition of the materials they are providing.

Even when the suppliers have the information, it isn't easy to get. Most purveyors are loath to pass on information to customers, treating their formulations as trade secrets. In many cases, it's akin to asking Coca-Cola for its secret formula. Rightfully, suppliers fear as well that information given for sustainability reasons could be used for nefarious ends, like reverse engineering to determine cost structures. Cost data could then be turned against a supplier in the next round of purchase contract negotiations. Managers often find that overcoming this suspicion requires breaking out of the traditional zero-sum, buyer-supplier relationship. Obtaining greater transparency requires higher levels of trust and partnership. True Textile's sustainability goals required a new buyer-supplier compact.

A good example of building such a compact comes from furniture manufacturer Herman Miller. In the late 1990s, Herman Miller began working with MBDC to integrate sustainability into its design process, requiring detailed analysis of the chemical composition of every material it used. The information needed for the analysis was controlled by Herman Miller's suppliers. The company's first attempt to get the data was a questionnaire faxed to the sales representatives responsible for the Herman Miller account. The response was dismal. At best, suppliers sent a copy of their standard MSDS back to Herman Miller. Others ignored the request completely.[17]

Herman Miller managers learned that they needed to sit down face to face with suppliers and build a trusting relationship. A good dose of legal protections like nondisclosure agreements also helped. The company spent over a year making presentations to its suppliers explaining its motivations. Getting the message across was often a time-consuming endeavor. The typical first response to Herman Miller's presentation was, "Why can't I just give you an MSDS, which is all I am required to do by law?" The company had to make clear that it was focusing only on the environment and not cost. Of course, the fact that Herman Miller is the number two company in the industry helped grease a lot of wheels, but the final decision to share the information was also facilitated by trust. Ultimately, fifty of the world's largest chemical suppliers agreed to participate in the Herman Miller initiative.

Smaller, less influential companies may have a harder time. True Textiles, a smaller player in its industry, found a carrot-and-stick approach was needed. The company held meetings with its suppliers and informed them that it planned to dramatically reduce its vendor count (the stick). Doing so, however, would mean that the company would be able to offer larger contracts to the selected firms (the carrot).[18] Times are changing, however, and green screeners have a new ally in their search for information: *regulators*.

The Return of Regulation

A new global regulatory power has emerged in the European Union. Because of its place as one of the top three global economic entities, EU regulations virtually apply around the world. Global businesses cannot afford to be shut out of the European market. In the late 1990s, the EU turned its attention to chemicals policy and began an effort to unify and update the existing patchwork of directives and regulations that had developed over time. In reviewing the existing system, the European Commission found that very little safety information existed for 99 percent of chemicals that entered the market prior to 1981. Of the over one hundred thousand chemicals in use in Europe, only three thousand had been tested, and of these, eight hundred were known to cause cancer or birth defects.[19]

To correct this information imbalance, the commission created the REACH directive (Registration, Evaluation, Authorisation, and restriction of CHemicals) in 2005, which will require greater disclosure, testing, and oversight. The legislation entered into force on June 1, 2007, and heralds a new regime for chemicals and materials management. While it will take until 2018 to be fully implemented, REACH imposes important changes on past practice, the first of which is to turn traditional responsibility for evaluating hazards on its head. European regulators reasoned that no one knows more about a company's products than the company itself. Thus producers, not regulators, have the responsibility to prove products benign by providing testing data that clearly establishes their safety. But responsibility doesn't stop with the producer. The EU regulations cascade responsibility down the supply chain to companies using materials in their production processes. Chemical customers are also required to consider the safety of the chemicals in their products and are expected to demand and receive the information they need to decide from the chemical manufacturers.

REACH has a number of critics, of course, especially in the chemical manufacturing industry. A report by the conservative U.S.-based Competitive Enterprise Institute (CEI) claims that REACH will create trade barriers that have a negative impact on companies around the world and will likely cost society "billions of dollars, reduce innovation and limit U.S. access to EU markets."[20] The European Commission, for its part, estimates REACH implementation will cost €2.8 to €5.2 billion spread over the eleven-year implementation time frame. In return, it also calculates Europe will save €54 billion in improved health and lower medical costs. Researchers from University College in London calculate substantially more savings over a thirty-year period, €284 billion.[21]

The impact of REACH will be felt by any company seeking to operate in the European market, but its influence will probably not stop there. The CEI report also sees efforts by the Organization for Economic Cooperation and Development (OECD) and the United Nations to make REACH a formal global standard, applicable around the world. Indeed, the UN has created the Strategic Approach to International Chemicals Management initiative in an attempt to coordinate global chemical and waste regulations.

There is action in the United States as well. Some U.S. states and members of the U.S. Congress are trying to create a REACH-like regulatory regime in the United States. In the summer of 2009, the American Chemistry Council, a trade group for the chemical industry, reversed a long-standing position and said it would support reform of U.S. chemical regulation with an emphasis on providing information to regulators about the health and safety impact of chemicals, significantly raising the likelihood of passage of new regulations.[22]

Greater materials transparency is thus on the horizon as green screeners get a hand from the EU's legislation and possible reform of U.S. laws. The data collected through the REACH process will be made publicly available through the newly created European Chemical Agency's Web site. The public will have, in effect, the right to contact manufacturers and ask questions about the makeup and associated hazards of their products. What's new is that manufacturers will be obligated to provide the answers to customer's questions.

The Impact of Green Screening

While not the original purpose of green screening, one of the positive outcomes is that it can foster greater materials parsimony. Because so little is known about the potential harmful impact of so many synthetic materials and the chemicals used to make them, precautionary green screening will yield a dramatic reduction in the number of materials acceptable for use in products. This impact can be seen clearly in the well-known case of Rohner Textile. The story of Rohner's award-winning Climatex Life-Cycle Fabric has become something of a legend in sustainability management circles, but what is often overlooked is the impact of the green-screening process on Rohner's suppliers. Beginning in 1993, Rohner used EPEA's screening protocol to evaluate the chemical dyes it used in fabric production. The project screened over sixteen hundred dye formulations from Swiss chemical giant Ciba-Geigy's portfolio and found that only sixteen passed its human health and eco-toxicity screens.[23] Sadly for Ciba-Geigy, screening eliminated 99 percent of its product line!

This is not an isolated incident. Since the initiation of True Textiles' green-screening effort, the company has screened over 151 products and approximately 280 individual chemicals. Only thirty of the screened chemicals have been approved for use in the company's new products.[24] Herman Miller managers echo this sentiment, "It is very difficult to find green materials."[25] These small-scale initiatives, however, portend bigger things to come as REACH takes hold. For its part, the European Union conservatively estimates at least three thousand chemicals will drop off the market as REACH comes fully into force.[26] I suspect history will show that to be a dramatic underestimate.

The Deeper Reason for Parsimony: Recycling

In general, companies don't green screen with the goal of reducing the number of materials used in their products. The motivation instead is risk mitigation, and in many cases, this impact of green screening came as a surprise to all involved. Thus, the materials parsimony emerging from green screening happens to be a fortuitous collateral benefit. There are important reasons, however, to go beyond toxicity and include an additional criterion in the materials-selection process: *recyclability*. The costs of forgetting recyclability can be seen in the spectacular failure of an ambitious public-private ecoproject known as Polyamid 2000.

In the late 1990s, carpet manufacturers were under fire from government regulators and environmentalists because over 95 percent of waste carpet was ending up in municipal landfills. With an estimated 5 billion pounds of waste carpet being dumped annually, regulators were considering banning the disposal of carpet in landfills.[27] Manufacturers had to respond, and in Europe they turned to Polyamid 2000, a huge carpet-recycling facility built jointly by the German government and private enterprises. Constructed on the site of a Communist-era manufacturing plant in the former East Germany, the facility was designed to recover waste carpet and recycle its materials, not only keeping carpet out of landfills but generating a profit by reselling the recovered materials.

By far the most valuable material in the carpet waste stream was Nylon 6 face fiber, which was estimated to make up 30 percent of all carpeting types in Europe. The value of Nylon 6 comes from its ability to be broken down chemically into its fundamental building blocks and then turned back into fresh material that is literally as good as the original, an idea we'll return to in chapters 2 and 3. And because nylon recycling uses substantially less energy, water, and other inputs than making virgin nylon from crude oil—in fact, over 90 percent of the material and energy originally used in making Nylon 6 can theoretically be recaptured in the recycling process[28]—Polyamid expected to be able to earn a profit on sales of Nylon 6 at market rates. Recycling other types of materials in the waste stream, such as wool and polypropylene, was more costly and found mostly lower-value applications and lower prices. Thus Polyamid would depend heavily on nylon for its profit potential.

The facility was a marvel of engineering, employing a highly automated assembly line for efficiency. Waste carpet was trucked into the plant and scanned to identify what it was made from: nylon, wool, and so on. It was then cleaned and transported on overhead conveyors to the recycling unit. Like panning for gold, carpet was ground up and put into tanks that separated the materials by buoyancy. The valuable nuggets of nylon that accumulated were sent on for further processing.

But despite the economic potential, the facility was bankrupt within three years. How could such a promising "green" solution fail so quickly? While it is hard to pin the facility's collapse on a single cause, one of the biggest problems was the proliferation of different materials in the carpet waste stream. Polyamid's managers were, in effect, digging through a mountain of waste carpet trying to uncover the valuable nuggets of Nylon 6 and extract them. Polyamid's managers were like miners quarrying for nylon ore. The costs of finding the nylon, which included trying to identify what the different waste carpets were made of, separating them, preventing cross-contamination, and processing them, proved too much. And the amount of usable Nylon 6 in the waste stream was far less than anticipated. There just wasn't enough to carry the accumulated costs of managing the whole waste stream. Choking on the proliferation of carpet material types, Polyamid was shuttered.

Polyamid's problem illustrates the hidden benefit of parsimony. One of the biggest costs of recycling is sorting and separating the chaotic mess of a waste stream. Materials parsimony enforces discipline on this mess and can dramatically lower overall recycling costs. If you choose the right parsimonious materials palette, it makes recycling easier and therefore more cost effective. German automaker Opel is a company that understands this. While most green screens are negative, by kicking out the undesirable materials, it is just as possible to create a positive green screen to proactively select preferred materials. Given this, Opel has created a priority list for positively selecting materials based on their recycling characteristics. As shown in figure 1-1, by combining both approaches, a small set of preferable materials quickly emerges at the intersection of the positive and negative screens.

How parsimonious can you get? VAUDE, a European sports-clothing company, has taken parsimony to the limit. While the

FIGURE 1-1

The small universe of materials parsimony

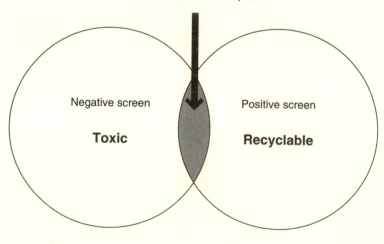

Parsimonious materials palette

Negative screen

Toxic

Positive screen

Recyclable

company has worked to get toxic materials out of its goods—it uses Switzerland's stringent bluesign screening process to ensure that its textiles are toxic-free—it has also pursued pure materials parsimony for other reasons. As part of an environmental strategy, the company began focusing on developing products that used fewer materials. VAUDE managers were able to identify one plastic—polyester—that could be used in a wide range of clothing applications. Working with its suppliers, VAUDE was able to obtain not just fabric and thread, but also hard parts like fasteners, zippers, cord grips, and everything else you need to produce outdoor clothing, all made from polyester alone. From this intensely parsimonious materials palette, VAUDE now produces an entire line of gear made from one material. The products extend from jackets to camping tents, all made from 100 percent polyester and with no sacrifices in aesthetics or performance.[29]

VAUDE did this, not for reasons of toxic hazard management, but to make the recycling of old garments and sports gear feasible. Think about trying to recycle a pair of jeans. First you'd have to separate any incompatible materials. Cutting the zipper free, for instance, would be labor and time intensive, probably making zipper recycling cost prohibitive. Furthermore, different types of threads are used to sew zippers and pockets onto the base material. If they are incompatible, attempting to recycle the garment whole could contaminate the recycling processes. But with homogenous products, like VAUDE's, there are no additional costs for separating, sorting, or screening materials at the end of their useful life. And there's also no risk of contamination. Tents, jackets, and sweaters all can be thrown into the same recycling process without concern. Considering the enormous savings from recycling materials like polyester and nylon, VAUDE's parsimonious palette has the potential to deliver both ecological and economic benefits. This is the real power of materials parsimony, creating the conditions for cost-effective recycling of materials.

Making a Buck on Parsimony

All this effort makes it seem that creating a nontoxic, parsimonious material palette is a costly endeavor, but the reality can be surprising. Supplier management and materials sourcing are often subject to the challenge of creeping complexity. In pursuit of top-line growth, companies continuously add "new and improved" innovations to existing products as well as whole new products. Often these decisions are not managed as part of an overall strategy but are instead taken on a case-by-case basis. The frequent result is a confusing proliferation of inputs and suppliers. Materials-screening efforts often reveal stunningly complex trees of bifurcating supply relations.

This complexity can carry hidden costs. Large manufacturers often have hundreds, even thousands, of supply relationships, and the costs add up. Just tracking the exception items on an accounting sheet is expensive and time consuming. Worse is the fact that many of these relationships are often too minor to result in an optimal pricing and sourcing marriage, generating unnecessary costs. Reducing materials-sourcing needs for parsimony reasons can thus have collateral benefits. True Textiles, for example, initially projected that green screening would increase chemical sourcing costs. Instead, the company netted nearly $300,000 in savings per year.[30] The savings emerged from the consolidation of its vendor base and the discounts from the larger volume purchases and reduced supply chain complexity. In short, most companies can find "low-hanging fruit" cost savings and efficiency gains to be had by decreasing the variety of inputs that go into making their products.

But legacy systems can stifle money-saving parsimony strategies. A leading pharmaceutical company, for example, learned that most of its chemical processes used solvents. Sustainability managers saw the opportunity to cycle the solvents from one process to another, multiplying their efficiency and cutting costs. But each of the processes had been developed independently by separate drug research and production teams. Each team had chosen a different solvent and was loathe to change, even though it could save substantial amounts of money and reduce the use of hazardous substances.[31] An overall strategy based on materials parsimony can overcome or eliminate many of these inefficiencies.

Beyond cost savings, some companies are finding materials-parsimony efforts a source of value-adding innovation. At the 2006 CERES Conference in California, for example, where Nobel Peace Prize winner Al Gore and other eco-luminaries were featured, a different kind of door prize was being handed out: bottles of S. C. Johnson's Windex Blue glass cleaner. Johnson was showing off its first product reformulated using its patented Greenlist chemical-screening process. In a twist on the marketer's old standby "New and Improved!" the company's vice president for global environment and safety was touting Windex's new formula as better for the environment. More important, it cleaned better than its predecessor and cost less to produce.[32]

Camper, the shoemaker founded on the Mediterranean island of Mallorca in 1877 by the Fluxà family of Spain, has also pursued its own innovative efforts to simplify the design and material composition of its products. In 1999, Camper undertook an initiative to create a novel, high-concept shoe that responded to the needs of nonsports customers as well the demands of the natural world. Beginning from Camper designers' observations that most people actually walk very little and spend nearly twenty hours a day inside in closed spaces, the Wabi design concept emerged. Described by one Camper designer as "an innovative shoe, healthy for people, clean for the planet," the name Wabi comes from Japanese meaning rustic, unpretentious, and inwardly oriented. To be "healthy for people," the Wabi was designed to be flexible and anatomically adapted primarily for indoor use. But the more innovative efforts came in creating a design that was "clean for the planet."

The shoe is made from just three components. The inner soles are fabricated from fully biodegradable Ramy wool or Igusa, which is the plant material used in Japanese tatami mats and can be easily removed from the shoe body. The flexible, outer shoe body proved challenging. Initially Camper designers had wanted to make it out of a bioplastic product, so that the whole shoe could be tossed into the garden and become compost at the end of its useful life. But the company could not find a supplier willing to work with it to create a biodegradable plastic that could meet the performance demands of a shoe. So the company turned to a single mold of the thermoplastic TPE, a material that was hard-wearing, flexible, and light. TPE is also recyclable. A combined focus on green materials and parsimony allowed Camper to produce a far simpler and more parsimonious product than nearly any other shoe on the market. The parsimonious design not only enabled future recycling efforts, it also saved money in both materials and manufacturing costs.[33]

Identifying value-creating benefits like these from materials-parsimony efforts is important. Reducing materials for sustainability reasons is the foundation on which subsequent steps are built. But it can also generate early wins in terms of cost savings or innovation that provide needed motivation and momentum to continue on to the next steps, the next biosphere rules.

That's where we'll turn now—moving from a parsimonious materials palette to rule 2: power autonomy.

2

Power Autonomy

Energy equals matter times the square of the
speed of light ($E = MC^2$).
—Albert Einstein

Einstein's brilliant theorizing led to his discovery of $E = MC^2$,
the seminal equation that resolved the mysterious relationship
between matter and energy. Like Einstein, companies seeking to
achieve embedded sustainability have their own matter-energy
problem to solve. Rule 1, materials parsimony, sets the foundation to sustainably address the material challenge. Rule 2, power
autonomy, attacks the other side of Einstein's equation: *energy*.

Power is important because every transformation of materials along Porter's value chain requires energy. Currently, about 90 percent of it comes from unsustainable fossil fuels.

Excessive global dependence on fossil fuels is a zero-sum competition that can cost business dearly. General Motors is a perfect example. Lulled into complacency by $16 per barrel oil in 1999, GM chose to simultaneously invest in the gluttonous Hummer and divest its pioneering EV1, the first modern-production electric vehicle. As GM shredded its last EV1 in 2003, gasoline began its rise toward $4 a gallon. In turn, the sales of GM's once profitable SUVs tanked, and, in sad irony, the post-bankruptcy company is making a last ditch, back-to-the-future wager on a new electric vehicle called the Volt. In contrast, its Japanese competitor Toyota began investing in gas-sipping hybrid technology when energy was still cheap. It has paid off. In 2007, Toyota surpassed GM as the world's largest-selling car company. GM, in contrast, was forced into bankruptcy. Of course, the 2007–2008 oil price run-up that put the company on the ropes is just a repeat of the 1970s oil shocks that gave Toyota a global foothold in the first place. Fool me once . . .

Or as British rockers The Who said, "Won't get fooled again." Even with a punishing global economic downturn, energy competition is set to worsen, driven by both unprecedented supply- and demand-side pressures. The International Energy Agency estimates that global demand will increase by more than 50 percent in the next two decades.[1] The World Energy Council, looking farther out to mid-century, foresees a need to double energy supplies by 2050.[2] It is unclear where all this energy, and the investment needed to make it possible, will come from. The dramatic fall in the price of oil in 2008 and the financial debacle have already caused many companies to put energy investments on a back burner. A situation that is setting us up for the next crunch.

The existing energy challenges have occurred with just 20 percent of mankind living an oil-rich industrialized lifestyle. But humanity is finally succeeding in extending the prosperity-generating benefits of business to the world's poor. China's economic miracle alone has done more to alleviate poverty than all the well-meaning international aid efforts combined; together, growth in China and India accounts almost entirely for the twenty-year decrease in the number of humans living in poverty. The global recession may set back Chindia's growth, but it will not stop it.

A growing middle class means growing energy demands. Currently, industrial world drivers burn close to 50 million barrels of oil a day, producing about a third of all climate-changing greenhouse gases. The world automobile fleet in 2003 was 540 million vehicles. But copying Western successes, the Chinese government is working furiously to build an automobile industry as a driver of economic growth. If China reaches a car penetration equal to Japan's or Europe's, 640 million additional cars would take to the road, an increase that would more than double the size of the current world automobile fleet.[3] That's just China. If the same occurs in India, the world will triple the car fleet in short order. These calculations can be extended to everything from toasters to TVs, each with its associated incremental increase in energy demand. Scientists agree that if this growth occurs through business-as-usual, we will choke on our fumes and bake in our greenhouse gases. In the meantime, we're certainly going to see highly volatile energy prices as demand grows much faster than supply.

Biosphere rule 2, power autonomy, helps companies to insulate themselves from the risks of convulsing energy markets,

TABLE 2-1

The business benefits of power autonomy

Biosphere rule	Business benefit
Power autonomy	Reduced energy costs
	Reduced compliance costs
	Reduced processing costs
	Improved environmental performance
	Improved customer performance
	Optimized for renewable energy

to create more appealing products for customers, and to save money. The benefits of pursuing power autonomy, as table 2-1 shows, are plentiful.

Nature's Way

When viewed from space, what differentiates Earth from other planets is the color: blue-green. The green that we equate with nature turns out to be chlorophyll, the substance within a plant that allows it to absorb energy from the sun. The sun is like a gigantic power station continuously throwing off terawatts of energy into the surrounding void. On Earth, it is growing plants that latch onto and use this flow to run the biosphere. The biosphere's inhabitants have metabolisms, which are the processes that convert captured energy and building-block materials into crawling and breathing creatures. And just as Einstein discovered for physics, energy and materials are intimately linked in biology.

When a deciduous tree, for example, emerges from dormancy in spring, it deploys hundreds of solar panels in the form of leaves. These panels harvest the solar flow for months and use it to build up the biomass that sustains and expands the tree. When the summer passes and the energy harvest ends, the tree unceremoniously dumps its solar panels on the ground. Within weeks (though not fast enough for most homeowners), those leaves are already decomposing, again becoming raw materials that will be used in next season's growth. The tree itself lives, dormant, off its stored energy sources.

When the sun is shining, power generation and use are simultaneous. But natural energy flows are inconsistent. Thus, storage becomes important for time-shifting generation and use. Life's growth and reproduction processes are adapted to the intermittent, renewable energy flows. Nature uses chemical batteries like sugars and fats to store power as part of the organism structure. Plants carry their energy technology within their structure: the form of the tree and its energy-generating and storage functions are combined. The saguaro cactus native to the Sonoran Desert where I live is a quintessential example of this integration. A cactus has no leaves. Its structure and power supply are integrated. The chlorophyll is not an add-on power source but is embedded in the structure.

The integration of energy technology with structure doesn't stop with plants. The Earth's flora capture the free energy spawned by the sun and then store it chemically as biomass and simple sugar. This chemical energy is then distributed to other animals and decomposers when they eat that flora as food. Through digestion, animals convert this food into muscle and bones, as well as fat. Like the tree's biomass, animal fat is just another way to store energy locally. When humans experience a food scarcity—either real or self-imposed through a diet—our bodies burn those fat stores.

Throughout the biosphere, energy-generation and storage processes are intimately integrated into the bodies of organisms. This integration depends on an initial outside source of energy (all of which eventually trace back to the sun) to feed it, but once captured and integrated into the structure of living things, that energy provides creatures with substantial autonomy. Most beings are not tethered to a power cord, but are free to roam, often in search of the next energy meal. The power autonomy of organisms provides the flexibility and mobility needed to ensure survival and reproduction in a changing environment.

Rule 2: Power Autonomy

The previous chapter addressed the material part of the sustainable production equation. But inherent in any production process is the other part of the equation: the use of energy to execute that process. Every transformation of matter in the manufacture of a product requires energy. Thus, energy inhabits all product design and production process decisions and is a key factor in the creation of a sustainable production system.

Unlike the cactus, which accesses the sun's energy, stores that energy in its green frame, and then generates its own energy by efficiently accessing those stores, industry to date has not found ways to economically access large quantities of renewable and emissions-free power to drive its processes. Nor has industry managed to use the energy it has had available in ways that are optimally efficient. This is true both for products and their production. The result has been an absolute and unsustainable power dependence on fossil fuels.

In nature, energy is used for three primary functions: metabolism, growth, and procreation. While business also performs similar functions, the biosphere analogy should not be too strictly interpreted here. What is important is that life has evolved using freely available, renewable flows of energy and has developed integrated systems to capture and store the often-erratic energy inputs.

For business, implementing rule 2 means integrating power autonomy decisions with product design and production processes from three perspectives: power efficiency, power generation, and power storage. By maximizing the power autonomy of products and processes, companies can move toward systems that function on renewable energy the way the biosphere does. In turn, they diversify their energy portfolio and begin to insulate themselves from risks of current and future energy market upheavals and impending regulatory restrictions on fossil fuels.

The Business Way

The power source for all living things is the sun's energy. Humans get their share of solar energy indirectly through the steak, potatoes, and salad we eat. The economy functions identically: cars, televisions, microwaves, and computers all feast on salad as well, but industry's salad is a bit different. It's fossilized. The oil, gas, and coal that account for over 90 percent of energy use in industrial countries are merely the petrified remains of the swampy carboniferous-era forests on which ancient creatures grazed. When those forests became extinct, they created, over millennia of decomposition and compression, a store of concentrated carbon-based fuel ready for exploitation. In effect, we are still burning firewood for our power; we're just burning much much older firewood.

This model is now facing real constraints, however. Energy analysts have been vigorously debating whether we have already reached a point of "peak oil," where our ability to economically increase production of oil ends. Peak oil doesn't mean that we've run out of oil, but that we can't *increase* the flow of oil into global markets. At the time I write this book, the world is currently pumping around 87 million barrels of oil a day. How much faster can we squeeze it out of the ground? No one really knows. But we do know that to produce more oil, we will have to discover new large reserves. Unfortunately, discovery of new oil deposits peaked more than forty years ago in 1968 and has been declining ever since. Unless geologists start finding huge new reserves quickly, and many argue that there are precious few left to find, our ability to increase production will dissipate.

While there is more oil to be had in the world's petroleum provinces, it comes with a constantly increasing price tag. The oft-discussed Canadian tar sands, for example, are supposed to hold the equivalent of a Saudi Arabia's worth of oil. But extracting it only becomes economical when prices exceed $70 per barrel. And that's before environmental externality costs like damage to the local environment and global climate change are calculated into the bill. Again, the problem is less about the actual quantity of oil but the cost of producing it. Most of the major new oil sources cost more than $60 per barrel to extract, and many planned investments in new capacity are only economically viable above $100 per barrel. When world prices are below $70 a barrel, capital investments from Mexico to Kazakhstan to Saudi Arabia are scuttled. At the same time, low gas prices have lulled consumers back into their old gas-guzzling habits. Witness the return of the Ford F-150 pickup truck as the best-selling car in the United States. The situation is setting up a new supply-demand collision that ends in only one way: higher fuel prices. If peak oil were the only concern, however, it might make sense to take a risk on business as usual. It's not.

Inherent environmental concerns aside, global climate change has become an important business issue because it is an increasingly important political and consumer issue. Until recently, politicians in general (but especially in the United States) have been hesitant to act. The so-called "skeptics" of climate change science have been able to cast enough doubt to shield politicians from action. That is no longer the case—whether the Copenhagen climate conference or Waxman-Markey cap-and-trade bill produce actually meaningful and workable regulatory schemes is somewhat irrelevant. While scientists may disagree about the impact of current levels of climate-changing greenhouse gases, they are essentially unanimous that the forecasted increases will be environmentally ruinous. As political action on climate-changing emissions becomes inevitable and other factors play havoc with energy markets, further upward pressure on fossil fuel prices can be expected.

The likely impact of regulation and shifting consumer attitudes means that, from a business perspective, the ongoing debate over the science is irrelevant. Regulation and consumer preference will force change regardless of managers' personal stance on the issue. Consider that Bob Lutz of General Motors, who called climate change a "crock of shit," in 2008 was also the driving force behind the aggressive development of the all-electric Chevy Volt.[4]

Of course, businesses can and should do much more than the minimum forced on them by politics and consumers. It's unlikely that any regulations put in place will be sufficient to reach the greenhouse gas emission reductions we would need to slow climate change. With even the direst predictions of the Intergovernmental Panel on Climate Change proving optimistic, some scientists have concluded that it's already too late to avoid major climate-change-related disruptions.

When confronted with facts like these, many managers struggle with their responsibility in the face of climate change. Unfortunately, there's no easy answer. At a minimum, as citizens we all have a responsibility to be informed about the science and the political process surrounding the issue. Admittedly, politics will largely decide whether or not we effectively address the current energy challenges. Energy is more a political commodity than an economic one, and energy markets are joined at the hip with government energy-infrastructure decisions. Nuclear and solar technologies are creations of government policy, not entrepreneurial risk taking. Biofuels, wind, and the much discussed hydrogen economy are the latest creatures of government policy.

On the supply side, the majority of energy resources are in the hands of governments, not businesses. And most oil-rich governments are organized into a market-hostile cartel called OPEC. Energy choices are therefore largely government choices. And it will be government policy that will ultimately decide our climate and energy future. But as leaders, executives have additional responsibilities, one of which is to guide their organizations through the impending changes successfully. The risks and opportunities are real. And this is where biosphere rule 2 comes in.

The Power Autonomous Organization

By acting like the biosphere, companies can both reduce energy risks and address environmental concerns through power autonomy. The rule of power autonomy is admittedly an ideal, like the political goal of energy independence, whereby companies decrease their reliance on increasingly volatile and environmentally damaging energy sources. Most companies can't achieve complete power autonomy today. Instead, power autonomy is a target to strive toward. The key metric that managers can keep in mind is percent of power autonomy (%PA), that is, the percentage of total energy needs derived from autonomous clean-energy sources. (The box, "The Power Autonomy Factor," explains the concept more completely.)

While the majority of businesses currently depend one hundred percent on centralized fossil fuel energy from external sources, new energy technologies like solar, cogeneration, wind, microturbines, fuel cells, and others are allowing companies to diversify energy supplies and even embed some energy generation into the organization itself. But investing in renewables to power existing processes that were designed with cheap fossil fuels in mind is a poor approach. Instead, managers need to pursue a simultaneous two-pronged strategy that begins by ensuring that energy use is optimized for renewable power sources. When combined with high-efficiency processes and facilities, renewable power helps companies move toward the model of power autonomy found in nature. Companies that have moved in this direction are finding immediate financial benefits. This is because power autonomy is like sending your company's energy system to the gym, making it more efficient, leaner, and cleaner.

Power autonomy can be pursued at three levels in the organization: (1) facilities and supporting business functions, (2) core production processes, and (3) a company's products themselves. While the core production processes are the real key to implementing the biosphere rules at the company level, this is probably the least developed of the three. We have a long way to go before

THE POWER AUTONOMY FACTOR

The pursuit of power autonomy is a process in which companies simultaneously pursue two interlinked paths, as shown in figure 2-1. The upper path is labeled the "Joe Ling efficiency curve," named after the 3M vice president Joseph Ling, sometimes called the father of pollution prevention, who inaugurated one of the first eco-efficiency programs at a major industrial corporation. This path is the systematic pursuit of greater efficiency in energy use and the reduction of power needs in business operations and products. The second, lower curve is the transition from fossil fuel power sources toward renewable alternatives. While both paths appear as straight lines in the figure, actual progress will not be linear but irregular, as the "lumpy" capital investments and innovations discussed in the chapter are implemented. The goal of the process is the eventual convergence of the two paths at a point of power autonomy, where a company and its products can meet power needs through autonomous renewable energy generation.

FIGURE 2-1

Paths to power autonomy

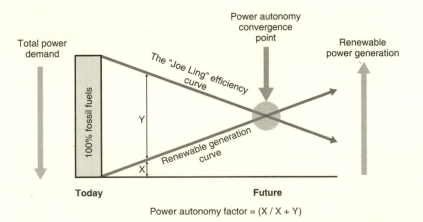

Power autonomy factor = (X / X + Y)

Progress toward the convergence point can be measured with the power autonomy factor, defined in the figure, which is the percentage of total power needs provided by renewable sources. An example of this is Google's 1.6 megawatt solar array installed at the Mountain View "Googleplex" headquarters in 2007. Google provides real-time data on its Web site about power generation, claiming current installations produce 30 percent of its peak energy demand and inviting the public to watch its ongoing progress.

production processes can become truly power autonomous, mostly because existing and long-lived manufacturing facilities were never designed to use energy from environmentally benign sources. Instead, the first places we are beginning to see actual power autonomy are in the corporate campuses and facilities around the world. I will therefore start there.

Power Autonomous Facilities

According to the U.S. Department of Energy, buildings account for 71 percent of electricity use in the United States and 38 percent of all greenhouse gas emissions. These numbers point to huge opportunities for improvement.

The frontier can best be seen in the newest sustainable building trend: green skyscrapers. Since the invention of steel frames in the 1880s, a skyscraper craze has driven corporations and cities to vie for the world's tallest building. The current holder of the title is the Burj Dubai which opened at the end of 2009. To hold contenders at bay, the Burj Dubai's builders are keeping its final height a secret until the tower is complete. Height may be passé, however, as a new race heats up to claim, not the tallest, but the greenest skyscraper. While cities like Moscow, Rotterdam,

Chicago, and even Dubai are all claiming the green skyscraper crown, New York City is generally credited as the site of the first green tower.

Built at 4 Times Square in 1995, the Condé Nast Building was a true pioneer. The tower today models partial energy autonomy by combining energy-saving lighting and cooling strategies with fuel cells and solar panels incorporated into the façade. When these green upgrades paid for themselves in three years, the business benefits of power autonomous office space were made clear to the world. The green innovations also helped the office space sell out far quicker than predicted. In fact, a 2006 survey by McGraw-Hill Construction found green buildings have higher occupancy and rental rates than their nongreen competitors. They also enjoy lower operating costs than the market average.[5] They are a top- and bottom-line win, and then some. When the grid went down in the 2003 New York City blackout, the Condé Nast tower became a beacon of power autonomy: it was the only lighted building in the darkened city.

A decade on, the Condé Nast Building is getting a greener neighbor. The $1 billion Bank of America Tower, located a block away, will be only the second tallest in Manhattan (after the Empire State Building) but is being lauded as a giant in green thinking. The tower will consume fifty percent less energy and water than traditional skyscrapers. The efficiency gains are achieved through "whole building design" that includes things like under-floor ventilation that can be adjusted for individual work spaces. The building achieves seventy percent power autonomy from an internal cogeneration plant and a thermal storage system in the basement that stockpiles cheap off-peak energy. Outdoor innovations include super-efficient windows and a green roof composed of heat-beating gardens and patios. It also incorporates a gray-water system that captures runoff and wastewater, reducing sewage discharge by ninety-five percent. The building's green gains could not be achieved without combining autonomously sourced energy with an energy-efficient infrastructure. The investment is also paying off in one of the worst commercial real estate markets in memory—as of the fall of 2009, well before the building was scheduled to open in 2010, the building was 98 percent leased.[6]

Outside of skyscrapers, the business benefits of power autonomous building design can make themselves known under strange, and sometimes strained, circumstances. When Texas Instruments (TI) went searching for a site for a new chip-fabricating plant in 2003, offshoring production to Asia looked like the only cost-competitive option. To make a similar U.S. plant cost competitive, and keep TI fabricating in Texas, the company would have to shave $180 million off the plant's $600 million construction and operating costs.[7] To TI's sustainability manager Paul Westbrook, it looked like an insurmountable problem, "like a bad dream."

Taking up the challenge, Westbrook sought the help of green building guru and energy expert Amory Lovins, cofounder of the Rocky Mountain Institute. Senior management at the firm was not initially enthusiastic about the collaboration, dubious that the outcome would be anything other than economically unviable suggestions. Instead, Lovins and Westbrook came up with power-saving changes that eliminated most of the traditional heating and cooling equipment as well as an entire floor of the plant needed to house the equipment. The changes cut building costs by 30 percent and reduced annual utility and water costs by over 20 percent. The company claims to save more than $4 million a year in ongoing costs because of the improved design. They also kept over one thousand jobs in the greater Dallas region. According to TI vice president of worldwide facilities Susan Sowell, "We exceeded a goal that we thought was impossible. How exciting is that?"[8]

TI's accomplishment is impressive, but today we are seeing the quest for power autonomy go beyond the single building or corporate campus. In the late 1990s, one of the first executive education programs I participated in involved training diplomats from the Middle East about sustainable energy development. At that time, oil was cheap, and it appeared there was an endless glut on the market. My job was to get the seminar participants to start thinking of economic development as a multigenerational effort that would require the creative destruction of current industries, including oil. To that end, I assigned them the task of imagining how to use petroleum revenues to foster new growth industries.

They came up with a smorgasbord of ideas: centers of excellence for health care and services; aquaculture; education and research. Some of the ideas seemed incongruent with the stereotypes Westerners have of Islamic countries: beach tourism, for example. Other ideas that seemed a stretch, like creating a financial center in the desert to rival New York or London, have since been fulfilled in the explosive growth of Dubai, Doha, and Abu Dhabi.

One team of participants took on alternative energy. In a post-petroleum world, their economies would need to find an alternative power source and growth driver. They proposed investing oil wealth in renewable energy technologies and turning the Middle East into the center for the clean power industry. Their plans included investment in research, manufacturing facilities, and building cities designed to run on nothing but the sun. They hoped to create an initial market for the technologies at home

that would help build solar energy into a viable global industry. It was an elegant, if unlikely, application of sustainable development thinking.

The surprising thing is that this vision is coming true in the emirate of Abu Dhabi. The oil-rich city state that controls 90 percent of the United Arab Emirate's oil reserves is investing $350 million from the Abu Dhabi National Energy Company to build a 500 megawatt solar plant. While impressive, the plant is just a part of the larger Masdar Initiative that includes the building of the first zero-waste, zero-carbon, and net-positive energy city— the first power-autonomous metropolis. According to Masdar CEO Dr. Sultan Ahmed Al Jaber the inspiration for the project came from the political father of the UAE, Sheikh Zayed bin Sultan Al Nahyan, who recognized that the Emirates were blessed with oil riches below, but also riches above in the form of abundant sunshine.[9] The Masdar Initiative is a multipronged effort to tap into these celestial riches, calling them "future energy," through the creation of a clean technology cluster in the heart of the Arabian Gulf. The project received a resounding endorsement in 2009 when the international community chose Masdar as the headquarters for the International Renewable Energy Agency (IRENA), the first new intergovernmental organization in decades and the first to be housed in the Middle East.

While the ambitions of Masdar and the financial resources employed are impressive, what is striking is the way Masdar is seeking to make power generation, business production, and human activity an integrated whole. Energy generation will not be something that happens at some distant plant with power transferred by a distribution grid. Instead, it will come closer to the saguaro cactuses I see everyday in Arizona: the integration of energy and production.[10]

Power-Autonomous Production

Inside corporate facilities are a company's production processes, which also need to be optimized toward power autonomy. Back when I was an environmental consultant, energy efficiency programs were part of many corporate eco-initiatives. These programs sought to reduce energy use and associated pollution in production operations. The classic example is 3M staff vice president of environmental engineering and pollution control Joseph Ling, who in 1975 proposed that line employees with intimate day-to-day knowledge of processes might be able to find efficiencies that senior management had overlooked. Ling's idea became the Pollution Prevention Pays, or 3P program, that invited employees to suggest projects that would reduce energy use or decrease operational waste. Somewhat skeptical, executives put a high hurdle rate on proposals: projects had to pay for themselves in one year.

In the first year, management agreed to fund twelve of the employee proposals. While results were positive, managers assumed that the twelve projects represented the low-hanging fruit, and the possibility of additional projects was slim. Still they ran 3P again. To their surprise, they got additional proposals, several of which were funded. There appeared to be more low-hanging fruit than expected. In fact, 3M has continued the program for more than thirty years. In a review for the thirtieth anniversary of 3P in 2005, the company counted more than six thousand employee-driven projects that improved the company's energy efficiency by 80 percent since 1973. Just as important, the projects reduced 3M's costs by over $1 billion, just in first-year savings. These projects are gifts that keep giving; those savings compound year after year. Recognizing that low-hanging fruit can grow back, 3M vowed in 2005 to double the number of 3P projects over previous years.[11]

If this was an isolated case, it could mean that 3M was just bad at cost management, with managers basically ignoring profitable projects. There are, however, other examples of companies that have initiated similar programs and generated comparable results. Dow Chemical launched the Waste Reduction Always Pays (WRAP) Award program in 1986, which followed a similar design, but also provided recognition and an award to employees whose projects were selected. Since its initiation, WRAP has completed 395 projects globally that have eliminated 230,000 tons of waste, 13 million tons of wastewater, and saved 8 trillion BTU's of energy. Dow calculates its total first-year savings to be around $1 billion.[12]

Despite these examples of success, when energy costs moderated in the late 1980s and early 1990s, many companies put energy efficiency investments on the back burner. But the turn of the millennium changed the landscape again, and companies became motivated to reduce their carbon footprints. In 2003, for example, Xerox set a goal of reducing annual carbon emissions to 10 percent below the 2002 rate by 2012. The company has already surpassed its target and saved an estimated $18 million, enticing Xerox to double-down on its bet with a new goal of a 25 percent reduction below 2002 levels in the same time frame.[13] DuPont took a slightly different tack and redesigned its products and production processes, creating a whopping 72 percent reduction in emissions, while generating savings of $3 billion.[14]

Savings can come from surprising sources. The logistics and delivery firm United Parcel Service (UPS), for example, decreased the amount of miles its fleet of ninety-five thousand trucks covered by an estimated one hundred million miles per year by simply eliminating the majority of left turns drivers made in a given day. This feat was achieved via the package-routing software the company uses in its in-truck computer system. Among other things, the software maps out the driver's daily route, not based on the shortest total distance but on the smallest amount of gasoline consumption. Thus it avoids left turns whenever possible, as research showed that idling while waiting to turn left accounted for a disproportionate amount of engine-on time. The resulting decrease in engine-on time translates into a savings of 14 million gallons of gas per year, a corresponding reduction of 130,000 metric tons in carbon emissions. The package-routing software program benefits UPS customers as well, as it allows UPS to reroute shipments to different locations, even when the driver has already begun the trip, and reminds the driver if he has forgotten to deliver a portion of the package.[15]

Whatever the motivation, projects like these take companies closer to the aspiration of power autonomy, where, if needed, the company could switch a significant portion of its energy generation to cleaner nonfossil fuel energy sources. However, while efficiency efforts push toward the goal, they frequently focus on making existing processes more efficient. Greater gains, however, may be found by rethinking our production processes entirely. Where industrial processes tend to grind, stamp, and cut material down to size, nature builds things from the bottom up. It does so elegantly in a water-based solution at atmospheric pressure and temperature, usually inside the body of a living creature. Nature's approach is based on atomic economics.

Atomic Economics

Nature manufactures at the micro-level, building an organism atom by atom. This process technology is key to the success of nature's elemental recycling efforts. Nature's biosphere rules are part of an interdependent system, and the linkages can be readily seen with rules 1 and 2. Rule 1 focused on the material side of the equation. Rule 2 focuses on powering the transformations of the selected materials. For businesses, therefore, material choices have a big impact on how well companies can implement the energy side of the equation. The two are interlinked because energy is integral in the transformation processes that turn raw materials into products and the process that recycles those products. Different materials have different abilities to be recycled into new value-added products. To be sustainable, material choices are therefore coupled with cost-effective recycling processes, something that few companies considered when designing existing processes. One of the key determinants of cost is the energy used.

Physicists will tell you that you can recycle almost anything if you throw enough energy at it. One famous example of just such an approach was the Massachusetts start-up Molten Metals Technology (MMT).[16] MMT was founded in 1989 by MIT-trained chemist Christopher Nagel and Harvard-trained entrepreneur Bill Haney. The pair made an explosive mix: Nagel had developed a patented technology that promised to address the hazardous waste problems of a broad range of industrial companies, and Haney, at age twenty-seven, was already a self-made millionaire.

MMT's technology was known as catalytic extraction processing (CEP), a technique that could theoretically take a stream of hazardous wastes, pass them through a 3,000 degree bath of molten metals, and break the waste down into its constituent elements. These elements could then be captured and recombined into industrial-grade raw materials for industry. If successful, CEP promised to recycle hazardous, radioactive, and toxic materials into benign chemical compounds and metals.

MMT's stock rose meteorically between 1989 and 1995, fueled by high-profile supporters, including Al Gore, who proclaimed CEP as a "shining example of American ingenuity, hard work, and business know-how."[17] The promise of the technology also attracted initial backing from big players like Fluor Corporation, Lockheed Martin, Hoechst Celanese, and DuPont.

By 1996, however, the company ran into trouble. In October, the U.S. Department of Energy cut off funding support for CEP. While the DOE official statement said the technology was sufficiently developed and no longer needed government support, the *Wall Street Journal* reported that in reality DOE experts had come to doubt the commercial viability of the technology.[18] This would be the company's undoing. While CEP had worked at bench and prototype scale, its corporate partners became disillusioned with its potential to work on a commercial scale. In commercial operations, the technology would face a hazardous waste cocktail that was far less controlled than the waste streams used in the R&D lab. By 1997, the company's stock price had collapsed, and the company filed for chapter 11 bankruptcy.

The problem with approaches like CEP is that they are predicated on replicating forces that happen naturally on this planet only deep in the earth's crust. The intense heat and pressure from such processes require huge amounts of energy. While replicating these approaches could potentially help address industry's sustainability challenges as far as materials go, they are a second-best approach compared to the way the biosphere works. Recycling, power generation, and use in nature are integrated within the bodies of living organisms, so they have to occur at nonthreatening, life-sustaining conditions.

In the absence of molten-metal-type technologies, materials choices become extremely important, because they largely determine the energy needed in reprocessing. Plastics are a good example. In terms of recycling, there are two important types of plastics: thermoplastics and thermoset plastics. Thermoplastics are formed into products by heating them and then molding them into shape. Most thermoplastics can later be reheated and molded into a new shape, thus enabling recycling. Thermoset plastics are different. When thermoset plastics cure and harden, bonding occurs within the polymer strands that make up the plastic and they irreversibly tangle together. The tangle can be undone only by breaking the strands apart and destroying the plastic. Trying to recycle this mess back into new material usually takes more energy than producing new materials from virgin inputs.

For material reprocessing to be economically sustainable, the selected process needs to produce recycled materials that are on par with original inputs in both functionality and price. Without this, they will have a tough time competing with virgin material inputs. This means that recycled materials must be cheaper than virgin materials, which depends predominantly on the energy needed to reprocess recovered materials.

Perhaps surprisingly, cheaper-than-virgin processing is not such an onerous criterion. Consider the fact that with recovered materials, much of the processing has already been done. A company that wants to make aluminum from scratch would first have to dig up bucketfuls of bauxite ore and pass it through a multistep, energy-intensive refining process. However, most of this costly upfront processing is eliminated when recycling aluminum cans, which are already a highly refined product. This is why recycling aluminum uses 95 percent less energy than producing the metal from virgin ores. It's a similar story for many other materials: recycling steel uses 61 percent less energy than new production; paper recycling uses 25 to 45 percent less; glass recycling uses 31 percent; many plastics range from 57 to 75 percent less.

New materials innovations in the coming years will open up additional alternatives that will best our current options. The emerging discipline of "green chemistry" is focused on improving chemical production and recycling processes and is already making intriguing discoveries. What is important for managers to keep in mind as they evaluate new and existing options is that the energy issue is a joint materials-process decision that links back to biosphere rule 1. Using the right limited palette of materials can inherently decrease the energy required to manufacture products. Of course, only part of the energy expended in manufacturing goes to materials processing. Another chunk comes from the energy used to assemble the article once the materials have been processed into usable form.

Solving the latter challenge is a frontier being tackled by U.K. department store Marks & Spencer. In 2007, the company announced its intention to become completely carbon neutral by 2012, a goal it intends to meet by relying solely on renewable energy for its business operations and the products it sells. Marks & Spencer's approach is particularly ambitious given that most companies usually tackle one or the other—operational efficiency or manufacturing efficiency. In pursuit of the goal, it has turned to its lingerie business. Marks & Spencer is the largest producer of lingerie in the U.K. market, with a 28 percent share in terms of production. In an effort to bring its lingerie production in line with its carbon-neutral goals, Marks & Spencer involved a manufacturing partner in Sri Lanka, MAS Holdings.

Founded in 1987 by a group of brothers, MAS Holdings has become one of the largest lingerie manufacturers in Southeast

Asia, with more than twenty factories and customers like Victoria's Secret and Nike, as well as Banana Republic, Gap, and Speedo. In April 2008, the company opened a new factory in Thulhiriya, Sri Lanka. Built with partial investment from Marks & Spencer, the express goal is having a carbon-neutral lingerie factory—probably the first of its kind. The plant has solar panels that provide 10 percent of its energy needs; the rest of the energy is grid-sourced hydroelectric, so that 100 percent of its energy consumption comes from renewables. The company also claims that the plant itself is 40 percent more energy efficient than comparable facilities, an efficiency gained in part through the use of innovative cooling methods instead of air conditioning. All this does come at a cost: the Thulhiriya plant cost 25 percent more to build than a nonenvironmentally friendly building of comparable size. The total decrease in energy costs will allow the company to break even on the higher cost of the plant in five years. This is not a vision of the future, but of a power-autonomous present. Marks & Spencer's green panties made their debut in June 2008.[19]

Power-Autonomous Products

Using power autonomy as a guide can help a company become more sustainable, efficient, and profitable. But it's not just buildings, operations, and manufacturing that need to move toward power autonomy. Power autonomy should also be a goal for the products a business makes. Power-autonomous products are those that can largely be un-tethered from a wall socket to some remote, centralized carbon-belching electricity plant. They are highly efficient in using and storing power, which enables reductions in emissions now and a switch to local, renewable energy sources or self-power in the future. Obviously, not many current products fit the bill.

Endless cheap energy has created a marketplace full of energy-wasting products. Take lighting, for example. Less than 5 percent of the energy stored in the coal processed in a power plant actually ends up as the light you need to read. Two-thirds of the original energy in the coal is lost in the electricity-generation process as waste heat. Another 10 percent or so is lost as the electrons travel long distances over the electric grid through sprawling powerlines. Even more is lost as heat in your incandescent light bulb. Likewise, only 2 percent of the energy in a gas tank is needed to move the driver; the remaining 98 percent is lost in combustion, friction, and motivating two tons of auto body down the road.

These designs have arisen because managers, designers, and engineers take an endless supply of cheap, reliable energy as a given. This convenience has frankly made them lazy when it comes to power consumption. Amazing things happen when you design as if cheap reliable energy supplies weren't there. In reality, for much of the world, it isn't. The U.S. Department of Energy estimates that there are 2 billion people in the world without electricity.[20] So what happens when you have to start designing products without cheap grid energy in mind? The founder of the MIT Media Lab, Nicholas Negroponte, found out.

In 2002, Negroponte announced the One Laptop Per Child (OLPC) initiative, an effort to make multimedia Internet-connected laptops, branded XO computers, available to millions of poor school children around the world. Known publicly as the "$100 laptop" project, OLPC has gained both admiration and derision. But the project has undoubtedly produced some exciting innovations in technological design. It had to. The target recipients of laptops were poor children in countries like the Democratic Republic of Congo, Bangladesh, and Nigeria, places where tens of millions of children live with no access to electricity. No electricity also means a digital divide without the connectivity the Internet provides to the larger world.

Of necessity, power was a major challenge for OLPC designers. Engineers therefore attacked the traditionally power-hungry laptop design elements like the screen, finding ways to reduce power consumption by a whopping 80 percent! To further save power, designers made it possible to switch the screen from back-lighting to a self-reflecting monochrome mode, which permits reading the screen in direct sunlight. These design changes meant that less heat was being generated, which allowed engineers to eliminate the cooling fan, saving even more energy. In all, the integrated power design allows the XO to potentially run for ten hours under hard use on a full battery charge and over twenty when it is in a more passive, backlit reading mode.

Pursuing product power efficiency to its full potential opens new options for power generation and use, even strange ones like "parasitic power." Anyone who has ever spent any time running on a treadmill may have wondered why the thing needs to be plugged into a wall to operate. Why hasn't anyone figured out how to tap into the power generated through all that human exertion to create a self-powered system that operates the machine and—depending on the power of the runner—an overhead light or an integrated television or radio? The dramatically reduced energy demand that OLPC engineers achieved allowed them to explore and ultimately choose this kind of human power. An early iteration relied on the power generated as users typed on the keyboard. A similar energy-capture strategy is exploited by the Toyota Prius hybrid car. When drivers press the brakes, the energy is captured in Toyota's regenerative braking system and sent back to the car's batteries for use when the stoplight turns green again. I ran into another example at a Rotterdam disco called "Watt" that runs its light show through the power of ravers bouncing on the club's energy absorbing dance floor.

In Negroponte's case, parasitic energy from typing turned out to be a bit too far out on the technological cutting edge, so instead XO users can charge their batteries using a hand crank, pedals, or a pull cord that works like a yo-yo. OLPC calculates energy generation in terms of a ratio: one minute of cranking provides ten minutes of use. The technology was popularized by London-based Freeplay Energy, a company founded to bring the benefits of power to the energy-poor developing world. Freeplay has built a range of human-powered products including flashlights and radios.[21] Of course, the XO can also rely on other sources like solar power or, assuming one is available and there's no brownout, the electricity grid. But low energy demand allows for greater flexibility and diversity in sourcing decisions. It permits autonomy.

The XO is an impressive technological achievement, but many of the innovations came from the need to design as if power were not cheap, reliable, and consequence-free. Products designed for base-of-the-pyramid consumers without access to reliable power are leading the way on power autonomy innovation. Virtually every week I see an announcement of a new solar-power LED lighting system or wind power–driven cellular tower. In each of these cases, like OLPC, the products have broader implications and applications than just use in the developing world. Negroponte and his engineers did not achieve the goal of a "$100 laptop," but the computer is currently in production and distribution at a cost of under $200. As the scale of production increases, costs will come down. OLPC didn't create the XO with an eye to value and power-conscious users in wealthy countries, but the existence of such a cheap, capable, and green machine is already changing the traditional laptop market. The current low-cost notebook computer craze is shifting the economics of the PC market and there is now talk of a "$10 laptop." The industry implications are yet to play out, but one thing is sure. The XO proves that complex, traditionally power-hungry technology products like computers can largely achieve the goal of power autonomy. And they can do it in cost- and feature-competitive ways. So why can't your product?

The Benefits

Integrating power autonomy into both business operations and products has myriad benefits beyond just cost savings. The one certainty about the future of power is uncertainty. Over the next decade, we will see mounting disruptions of cost and availability as traditional sources of energy become constrained and governments around the world force myriad changes in the way we create, consume, and pay for power. Becoming more power autonomous will help insulate companies from the upheaval and risk of a rapidly changing energy environment. Power autonomous products will likewise become favorites of customers, whether consumers, other businesses, or the government, for the exact same reasons. Witness the enthusiasm for hybrid and electric cars among consumers, Boeing's fuel-efficient 787 Dreamliner among airlines, and parasitic power systems for troops that capture the energy of a soldier's movements to power technologically sophisticated weapons systems from the U.S. military.

Power autonomy, when combined with materials parsimony, creates the opportunity for economically turning the value chain into a value cycle, which is rule 3 of the biosphere and the subject of the next chapter.

3

Value Cycles

RULE 3

Recover and reincarnate materials from end-of-use goods
into new value-added products.

---

*That all things are changed, and that nothing really
perishes and that the sum of matter remains exactly
the same, is sufficiently certain.*
—Sir Francis Bacon

The value chain model has long served the needs of business production, but today we know it is built on faulty assumptions
about what happens at both ends of the chain. On the upstream,
input side of the value chain, the assumption was that inputs
would always be abundant and cheap. While prices may fluctuate
wildly, global resource demand is trending ever upward. The

emergence of middle classes in China and India alone will quickly triple the demand for goods and the natural resources needed to make them. At the same time, as demand accelerates, supplies of resources around the globe are tightening, making inputs of everything from oil to water costly and scarce. On the output end of the value chain, the assumption has been that the environment can limitlessly accept consumer and industrial waste. It can't. Even at current levels of economic activity, evidence indicates that the Earth's systems are overtaxed. With pressures increasing at both ends, the value chain model will have to change.

In many industries, from automobiles to electronics, change has already begun. Governments are demanding that companies deal with the full life cycle of their products, known variously as product take-back, total producer responsibility, extended product stewardship, or end-of-life legislation. Regulations like the EU Package Waste Directive or cell phone take-back legislation in California and New York are compelling businesses to recover their old goods. Companies that try to recycle the reclaimed products without changing their value chain model will have a mess on their hands. You can't just bend an existing value chain around on itself and hope it spontaneously forms an economically viable value cycle. For those who implement rules 1 and 2, however, the basic foundation of a profitable value cycle has been set, and executives will find that their investments in materials parsimony and power autonomy mean that the recovery of their end-of-life products can become an economic boon for the company.

Where Nature and Industry Diverge

Everything we see is made of recycled stardust. A romantic image, perhaps, but true nonetheless: all the elemental materials in the universe, including those found in the human body, were fashioned following the Big Bang. Within minutes of the Big Bang, the first elements began cooling out of the livid, expanding plasma. Hydrogen was one of the first to form, followed by other elements including life-building carbon, oxygen, and nitrogen. On Earth, several billions of years after the Big Bang, these materials were caught up in biological cycles that allowed them to be reincarnated over and over into constantly evolving life forms. From the first single-celled protozoa to a modern-day African elephant, the biosphere has simply reused the same materials repeatedly in constantly shifting and evolving configurations.

Nature's biological cycles are driven by the actions of the Earth's organisms themselves. It is through the act of living, growing, consuming, and dying that the cycles turn. Ecologists categorize organisms according to the role or ecological function they play, dividing life into *producers, consumers,* or *decomposers.* Producers are the foundations of ecosystems. They take up raw materials from the air, water, and earth and fashion them into growing plants. As we explored in rule 2, building a tree out of thin air, water, and dirt requires energy, and producers generate it by tapping into the free flow of solar rays constantly bombarding the planet. Consumers, in turn, graze on the producers to extract their captured energy and materials, which funds their own metabolism and growth. Finally, decomposers release the residual energy stored in dead plants and animals and return their constituent materials to the earth, where they become the inputs for a future generation of producers. This system of production, consumption, and decomposition allows life's parsimonious palette to cycle over and over in an ongoing process of evolution.

Commercial manufacturers, in contrast, focus solely on the production phase, orienting their businesses along throughput

TABLE 3-1

The business benefits of value cycles

Biosphere rule	Business benefit
Value cycles	Input cost savings
	Reduced processing costs
	Reduced supplier risk
	Increased control over brand and reputation
	Improved asset management
	Improved customer information

value chains, operating in a one-way flow from natural resource extraction to the dump. With value chain thinking, what happens to the product after sale is traditionally none of the manufacturer's concern. However, the implementation of rules 1 and 2 changes the game. Companies that design products using a parsimonious number of nontoxic materials that are linked with energy-efficient recycling processes will quickly find they have a vested interest in getting those end-of-life products back. The products morph from simple, valueless waste to an economically valuable supply of inputs for the next production run. This is biosphere rule 3: fashioning your materials palette and processing technologies into a viable value cycle. For the companies that have implemented value cycles, the reward has been growing profitability and greater environmental sustainability (see table 3-1).

Rule 3: Value Cycling

Humans have long tapped into nature's preexisting biological cycles for our own production needs. Natural fiber textiles, leather goods, and other plant and animal products are all examples of humankind's surfing of biological cycles. While we continue to do so, the domination of modern industrial methods poses problems for natural cycles. The biosphere has no processes for breaking down the majority of our synthetic chemicals, some of which are poisonous to ecosystems. This lack of natural capacity requires that we create the equivalent of biological cycles for most of our modern high-tech materials. My colleague William McDonough argues that the biological cycles of nature must be augmented with man-made technical cycles for industry. Companies' next practical step toward sustainability is to emulate nature's biological cycle in a business value cycle.

Admittedly, we cannot currently replicate nature's ability to break down and build up organisms at a molecular level. For this reason, the business application of value cycling diverges a bit from nature. Instead of nature's atomic-level recycling, industry value cycles can be created at two distinct levels, something that can easily be understood by thinking of product manufacturing hierarchically (see figure 3-1). The base of the hierarchy is the *materials* that comprise a company's parsimonious palette. Materials are, in turn, fashioned into parts or *components* that are the submodules that perform different functions of a product. Components are then assembled into the final *products* that are sold to customers. A car, for example, is a product assembled from components such as engines, wheels, and windshields, which are in turn made from materials such as metals, plastics, and glass.

Value cycling strategies are built at one or both of the two levels of the hierarchy: the components and/or the materials level. Component cycling—often called reuse, refurbishment, or remanufacturing—allows current product designs to be recovered and cycled back through multiple sales to different customers.

FIGURE 3-1

Product manufacturing hierarchy

Product hierarchy

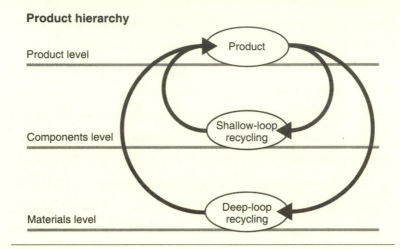

This strategy is found in some durable goods industries like aviation and capital equipment. Material cycling, in contrast, allows the more fundamental materials to be reconfigured into new product designs. Material cycling is most often equated with activities such as glass, metal, and paper recycling. Energy is required to power a process that unzips the materials from their current configuration, freeing them up to be rezipped into new products. This is why pursuing parsimony and power autonomy in production and processing technologies, as discussed in the preceding chapters, is an important preceding step to value cycling.

Materials are turned into components, and components become products. Recycling can be done just at the component level, called shallow-loop recycling, or at the materials level, called deep-loop recycling.

Value cycling at different levels of the product hierarchy can be seen in figure 3-1. The inner or "shallow-loop" is recycling at the components level. In shallow-loop cycling, products and their components are recovered and restored so that they can be used again in their original configuration. Think of the various goods you can buy that have been "refurbished," or the recycling of printer toner cartridges. Shallow-loop cycling is about extracting the maximum value from an original investment in a product asset. It's about maintaining the quality and use of already-built products, passing that usefulness along to a new customer, while at the same time profiting from an additional secondary sale. The outer or "deep-loop" is value cycling at the more fundamental materials level of the hierarchy. Here, products and components are decomposed into their original constituent materials. Those materials are then reintegrated into the production process as raw material input and emerge as new, different, and, ideally, superior products. Deep-loop value cycling is about fostering innovation and allowing product lines to evolve to the next superior design generation. Depending on the product line, companies can utilize both shallow-loop and deep-loop value cycling.

Shallow-Loop Value Cycling

The well-known Kodak "one use" disposable cameras provide insight into the value of shallow-loop recycling. Driven by a combination of business opportunity and environmental concerns about camera waste, Kodak built a shallow-loop reuse system that cycles its disposable cameras up to ten times. The company's program collects used cameras that have been returned to photofinishers and transports them to a central facility where they are sent to one of Kodak's manufacturing plants for refurbishment. The cycling begins by removing the front and back covers and inspecting the cameras thoroughly. They are then reloaded with fresh film, covered with new outer packaging, and sent back to retailers to await the next purchase. As a consequence, the company gets up to ten sales from the same asset, not a bad proposition. With nearly one billion cameras reused to date, Kodak claims to produce 90 percent of its manufacturing volume from recovered cameras alone.[1]

While little recognized, the scale and value of this type of shallow-loop remanufacturing is impressive. By some accounts, the remanufacturing industry employs the same number of people and produces about the same economic turnover as major industries, like the $170 billion pharmaceutical sector. Household names such as General Electric, Caterpillar, Boeing, John Deere, Pitney Bowes, and others are estimated to collectively remanufacture $130 billion in products each year.[2]

During my graduate studies in 1995, I took Harvard Business School's environmental management course in which we studied one of the first cases of successful shallow-loop value cycling: Xerox Corporation. The case, written by HBS professor Richard Vietor, has become a classic.[3] It tells how, by abandoning the "sell it and forget it" mentality of value chain thinking, Xerox extended the concept of a corporate asset from the traditional equipment and inventory found at its facilities to include its printers and office equipment installed on customer premises. The company then began to actively manage this installed base as part of an overall value cycle, employing shallow-loop remanufacturing techniques. While there were obvious environmental benefits to the asset management approach, company executive Jack Azar argued from the beginning that the strategy's intent was economic competitiveness, not sustainability. Given that the company reduced costs by $64 million in the first three years of the program, it seems that Xerox succeeded. But the untold story of the true competitive potential of Xerox's idea can be found, not in the United States where Xerox is headquartered, but on the other side of the world, in Australia.

In 1962, as part of its international expansion, Xerox created a joint venture with Fuji Photo Film to sell its xerographic products in the Asia-Pacific region. Over the intervening years, Fuji acquired a 75 percent stake in the venture, which became known as Fuji Xerox. By the early 1990s, however, Fuji Xerox in Australia was in trouble and losing money. The business was running at a loss due largely to the cost of importing parts from overseas, which were the biggest expense on the company's P&L statement. The board of directors was desperate to return to profitability and was willing to consider nearly any out-of-the-box idea that could turn the company around. They found just such an approach championed by Dan Godamunne, an engineer who had once worked in Xerox's R&D department in Rochester, New York.

In early 1992, the Fuji Xerox board invited Godamunne to make a presentation. He recommended an asset management-based value cycle approach that would remanufacture the high-cost components that were coming from overseas and draining the company's treasury locally. Board members were skeptical about Godamunne's ideas and uncertain about the economics of the approach. By Godamunne's own admission, the directors saw him as "a mad rocket scientist," but because of the company's dire straits, they had nothing to lose and gave him a shot.

Godamunne's early research indicated that there was low-hanging fruit. For example, he found that almost 50 percent of the supposedly "faulty" units quickly swapped out by field service people trying to minimize customer downtime were perfectly functional. Better diagnostic tools helped deal with this problem but only addressed the recovery of functioning assets. Godamunne saw that new diagnostic tools could go much farther. By more accurately pinpointing the problems in returned assets, diagnostics could streamline the remanufacturing process. Godamunne employed a technique called "signature analysis" to measure a product's current performance and compare it against the performance of a brand-new unit. Doing so could accurately forecast the future functionality and potential breakdown of the unit. Like a doctor, Godamunne's diagnosis identified which of a product's component "organs" were fit and which were ailing. The signatures proved so accurate that Fuji could even predict what percentage of "useful life" remained in a product before remanufacturing was needed. This information would give Fuji Xerox the confidence to offer its customers full warrantees on remanufactured units that were actually less risky than new product warrantees.

With data in hand, Godamunne went back to the board of directors and presented his value cycle strategy. This time the board was sold and got fully behind the effort. Fuji Xerox began value cycling in earnest in 1993, and just two years later the company made an operating profit. Thanks largely to Godamunne's value cycling strategy, for the first time in ten years Fuji Xerox was competitive in Australia. The success is easy to understand when you look at the economics of a component like the laser used in a laser printer. Before value cycling, Fuji Xerox had to purchase lasers new from its suppliers for about $14,000. But today, using its value cycling approach, Fuji Xerox can remanufacture a laser recovered from its own installed base of printers for less than $2,500. Within a handful of years, a full 40 percent of the company's total bottom-line profit was coming from remanufacturing and service efforts. It is not an overstatement to say that shallow-loop value cycling saved the company.

Godamunne eventually became general manager of Fuji Xerox's Eco-Manufacturing Centre, a facility dedicated to remanufacturing Fuji Xerox parts and components not just for Australia, but for the entire Asia-Pacific region. Opened in 2000, the center today remanufactures more than two hundred fifty thousand parts each year. The economic benefits for Fuji Xerox are impressive, but the sustainability benefits are equally notable. The Eco-Manufacturing Centre works as a zero-landfill facility with only a half of 1 percent (by weight) of products passing through ending up in a landfill. Everything else becomes a resalable product at a cost much lower than producing new components. The center's environmental achievements have been honored by organizations such as the United Nations and the Australian Institute of Engineers.[4] The eco-adulation is obviously welcomed by Fuji Xerox, but executives will admit the driver from the beginning was purely economic. According to Godamunne, "We say what is good for the environment is good for business, but for Fuji Xerox, it started out the other way around."[5]

Obviously, the benefits of shallow-loop value cycling are not limited to printers. General Electric is another company that has exploited the power of the value cycle. In 2001, for example, GE units in the energy, transport, and medical industries generated nearly a third of their revenues from shallow-loop reuse of products and components. GE developed its shallow-loop strategy by expanding its vision of product servicing under the leadership of Jack Welch. During that time, the company moved beyond parts replacement to the systematic management of GE products installed at customer sites. Such potential exists elsewhere as well. In fact, a standard rule of thumb holds that materials account for 70 percent of the cost of building a product. By recovering materials and components at a fraction of the new price, shallow-loop cycling can dramatically reduce costs. In many cases, remanufacturing a product costs 40 to 65 percent less than producing it new.[6]

While the potential economic benefits are significant, there are obvious environmental advantages as well. Research shows that shallow-loop reuse shaves product and process energy use by at least 15 percent and often much more. Photocopier remanufacturing, for example, requires 20 to 70 percent less energy. Remanufacturing also translates into impressive increases in asset productivity and potentially huge raw material savings. At current levels of remanufacturing, it is estimated the United States saves 16 million barrels of oil a year and avoids 28 million tons of carbon dioxide emissions.[7] One recent study indicated that widespread use of remanufacturing could reduce material consumption and waste creation by a factor of three.[8]

Choosing whether a shallow-loop value cycle makes sense for a given company will depend on the unique circumstances of the product, assets of the company, and the marketplace. Shallow loops do not make sense for all products. Durable, modular products that have long life cycles, such as capital equipment, trucks, appliances, and so on tend to be good candidates. In a survey of over twelve thousand existing remanufacturers, Boston University professors William Hauser and Robert Lund showed eighty-three different product categories, but found that capital equipment and transportation dominated.[9] Products where technological changes are rapid, like electronics, or where rapid shifts in fashion occur seem less amenable to a shallow-loop process.

Where possible, the logic of shallow-loop value cycling is spreading, especially when commodity and energy prices rise. Companies that have pioneered the approach are now seeing opportunities for replicating their success in other sectors. The industrial equipment company Caterpillar, for instance, has extensive remanufacturing expertise developed over a thirty-year period. The company is now leveraging that expertise in new industries. Caterpillar has begun acquiring small and medium-sized independent firms already involved in aftermarket remanufacturing as part of a roll-up strategy. In 2006, for example, Caterpillar bought Progress Rail Services Corporation, an Albertville, Alabama, company that services and remanufactures railcars. Since then, the company has branched into power products and fuel systems and continues to scan the market for new acquisitions.[10]

Fuji Xerox's Dan Godamunne tells anyone who listens that the profitability of his approach in not just a concept, but a proved fact. When asked if the ideas are applicable across a broad spectrum of industries, his answer is an unhesitating, "Absolutely." According to Godamunne, "We developed techniques for the motors and electronic components in our printers, but the approach is applicable to all such components in any industry. Can you tell me an industry where you won't come across a motor or electronics?" Godamunne and Fuji Xerox are launching efforts like a joint venture with Ford Motor Company to apply the technology, techniques, and thinking to the automotive industry. "The implementation challenge for companies," says Godamunne, "is a matter of priority, not possibility."[11]

Challenges to the Shallow Loop

While promising, there are obviously challenges in establishing a shallow-loop value cycle. In most places, remanufacturing is still more art than science. Many shallow-loop cycling operations are reminiscent of the early days of car building when automobiles were produced by artisans, one at a time. Shallow-loop cycling tends to be more labor intensive than traditional manufacturing, and because disassembly often requires a trained eye and hands, the type of labor needed is usually skilled. All this means labor costs for shallow-loop cycling can be higher than assembly line manufacturing. However, while labor accounts for about 30 percent of production costs on average, the labor cost increases are offset by the potential 70 percent materials savings coming from recovery. Thus, the economics are often attractive, even with higher labor costs.[12] Over time, however, as advances in remanufacturing technology develop, techniques become widely known, and product design improvements are incorporated, shallow-loop cycling will become increasingly streamlined and efficient. A big profitability prize awaits the future Henry Ford of shallow-loop value cycling.

In addition to labor costs, companies that engage in shallow-loop cycling like Fuji Xerox may have to face a problematic stigma. Until now, remanufactured products have been seen as secondhand and, by definition, of lesser quality than the originals. This impression is often reinforced by pricing policies that sell remanufactured products at a 30 to 40 percent discount off their "new" siblings. The reputation is often tied to the "sell it and forget it" mentality of value chain thinking. In a value chain, the seller hands the product to the customer with a smile and a wave and abandons it. In that scenario, a recycled or refurbished product seems to be of obvious lower value. So even with a warranty, customers have been subtly trained to expect some kind of compensation for taking on the perceived risk of a "used" product. In the case of remanufactured goods, this compensation has historically come in the form of lower prices.

But when done correctly, remanufactured products don't perform worse than new products. According to Fuji Xerox's Graham Cavanah Downs, "The way we're re-manufacturing here is really a total change in concept. It's a paradigm change in that components of our equipment are re-manufactured to a standard which is always as good as if not better than new."[13] Dan Godamunne raised eyebrows when he told the press that "not only can we remanufacture parts to the same quality as new parts but we can remanufacture parts to *better* quality than new parts."[14] Because Fuji's analysis allows it to learn what will bring on critical failures, it can attack the weaknesses of the original design in remanufacture and enhance the component's and the whole product's life.

Some companies have begun to see value cycling as a competitive weapon. In 1986, for example, Hill-Rom, the market leader in advanced hospital beds, created a new business division called HBR Healthcare to refurbish older, electric hospital beds. The company developed a multistep restoration process to produce hospital-grade beds at a very competitive cost. As the industry leader, Hill-Rom's market share, production cost advantages, and reputation provided excellent access to used beds, an advantage that was enhanced by being the first among its competitors to pursue shallow-loop cycling. The company offered the beds to its health facility customers at substantially lower prices as part of a package of other products and services. HBR Healthcare was so successful that its rivals resorted to suing the company on antitrust grounds, arguing the refurbishing strategy was really an anticompetitive move and not motivated by a legitimate business concern. Clearly the competitors could not contend with the cost advantage of $2,000 for a high-quality refurbished bed when their new beds cost $6,000 to $10,000.[15]

Today, HBR Healthcare continues to recover and value cycle used hospital beds and seems well positioned as hospitals and governments look for ways to trim health care costs.

As the performance difference between new and used components disappears, companies can think strategically about how to price their remanufactured goods. Some companies, for example, are pursuing a strategy known as "dual sourcing," meaning that product components can be sourced interchangeably from new or recovered sources. Any given final product can have a mix of new and refurbished components. Companies like Xerox and the Dutch maker of printing equipment, Océ Technologies, have already moved to dual-sourcing models.[16] When this is done, the difference between new and used fades and allows companies to capture higher margins from their refurbished products or use lower prices to capture market share without having an impact on profitability.

Deep-Loop Value Cycling

Shallow-loop cycling can be an important advance, both economically and environmentally. But sustainability isn't about one or even two product generations. Sustainability is an intergenerational strategy. Doing it right means not having to worry about the environmental implications for our lifetimes, or our descendant's lifetimes, or our descendant's descendant's lifetimes. Sustainability in nature has worked for hundreds of millions of generations. While managers may not need to think about planetary time frames, thinking about our great-grandchildren should be part of standard operating procedure.

Managers who embrace this logic will confront a fundamental truth: no matter how effective a company's shallow-loop reuse system works, it will still need to have a deep-loop value cycle strategy. There are two reasons for this. First, even the best-built components and products eventually wear out, despite refurbishment. Over time, all components abrade, erode, or corrode. This gradual dissipative loss is inevitable; the third biosphere rule can't trump the second law of thermodynamics. At some point, a product or component can no longer be remanufactured to a high enough standard, and without a deep-loop value cycle, it becomes trash.

The other issue is simply progress and change. Many companies have become expert at building durable long-lasting products. My 1997 Toyota Corolla, for example, is an incredibly reliable car. It is so well designed and of such high quality that it continues to operate without problems with nearly a quarter of a million miles on the odometer. I don't see that changing soon. But Toyota is continuously innovating and improving its vehicles, adding new features, safety devices, and other design changes. This makes it more likely that I will upgrade to one of Toyota's hybrid Priuses before my Corolla breaks down for good, especially if gas prices stay high. Because products are always evolving and improving, and market conditions are constantly changing, companies need a sustainable materials strategy that can accommodate progress and bring the products and components through an end-of-life or end-of-use process.

A new version of planned obsolescence needs to be adopted as a fundamental design consideration. This needs to be done with care, however, given the stigma associated with planned obsolescence in the past. In the 1960s, U.S. car manufacturers were crucified by environmentalists and consumer advocates for their version of planned obsolescence. Their goal at the time was simply to sell more cars and keep manufacturing plants operating at optimum capacity. To do so, the Big Three auto manufacturers made constant, sometimes small, changes to body styling and trim. A little chrome here, a fin there. The automobile became a fashion statement that, like clothes, could change with the seasons. And it worked. Customers, on average, were buying a new car every three years. But success had its critiques. Carmakers were even accused of nefariously building accelerated failure rates into their products, all in an effort to force customers to speed up their buying cycles.

In nature, however, obsolescence, also known as death, is essential to keep the biosphere running. But more important, it makes change and evolution possible. Obsolescence of products is likewise inevitable and, if done correctly, can be seen as desirable from the perspective of the client, the producer, and even the environment. Deep-loop value cycles are about reincarnating materials into new and improved products, upgrading their quality of use to better evolve with the needs of your customers. It is an evolution-enabled strategy of innovation and progress.

While shallow-loop cycling offers a lot of short-term opportunities, deep-loop value cycling is an essential part of reaching the sustainability destination. Once you have a shallow-loop value cycle in place, you'll need to consider how to add on a deep-loop cycle as well. Kodak, for example, has both cycles in place for its disposable cameras. After a certain number of loops, the plastic components in its cameras inevitably fail quality and performance testing. When this happens, they are separated out and sent to a third-party recycling center where the plastic is reprocessed and remolded into new camera parts.

Deep-Loop Value Cycle Design

Deep-loop value cycle design allows materials to be recaptured and reinserted into new high-quality products. In an ideal world, business could just replicate nature's technology for recycling our synthetic materials. But recycling in nature occurs at the elemental level, using nano-scale processes to break down and build up organisms, atom by atom. Our current technology is not up to the task of nano-scale recycling (though we may live to see it happen). Right now, however, only companies that make products out of natural materials like plant and animal fibers can rely on biological processes to decompose and recycle their end-of-life products. There are design caveats, of course. The products have to be 100 percent biodegradable and not mixed with nondegradable or toxic synthetics.

Innovative biologically based materials, like bioplastics, are on the horizon, and many companies are experimenting with naturally derived inputs. Again, if these materials are correctly designed, they can rely on nature's processes for recycling. However, while many bio-based materials do break down, they often do so very slowly, if at all, unless under special conditions. We are not yet at the point where customers can plow their old bioplastic blender into their tomato garden and forget about it. In many instances, decomposition times of six months or less requires the use of a commercial or industrial composting process. Because of the need for specialized processes, companies that rely on bio-engineered materials and processes will need to consider deep-loop value cycle design in much the same way as companies with synthetic materials.

Designing a deep-loop value cycle is simplified when materials parsimony and power autonomy have already been pursued, but it does require an additional change of mind-set. Instead of viewing end-of-life products as waste that someone else must dispose of, companies will need a capacity for reacquiring the product and deconstructing it into its usable, extractable materials. Businesses that have expended significant effort in selecting a parsimonious material palette will have an incentive not to lose those materials at the end of a product's useful life.

A good example of deep-loop value cycle design can be seen at Shaw Industries, a commercial carpeting company. Shaw manufactures carpet tiles, the flat squares traditionally used in office buildings around the world. Carpet tiles are made of a soft face fiber surface that we walk on and a heavy backing material, much heavier than that used for residential carpet, that holds the carpet flat. In the late 1990s, Shaw was dealing with the same government and interest group pressures that led to the founding of Polyamid 2000 (discussed in chapter 1). Steve Bradfield, senior vice president for the environment, who led Shaw's response, requested a million dollars in R&D funds from senior management to develop the "carpet of the twenty-first century."[17] Bradfield proposed a pilot production line to experiment with a new nontoxic carpet backing that could be fully recyclable into new backing. His idea was that by pairing a nontoxic backing with face fibers made of Nylon 6 (the plastic, described in chapter 2, that can easily be broken down and recycled), Shaw could create a product that was energy efficient, nontoxic, and deep-loop recyclable. If successful, Shaw would be able to recover its customers' waste carpet and recycle it into new, high-value flooring, thus doing away with the landfill problem. Bradfield could provide his superiors no guarantees of technical success. Nor was he, or anyone else for that matter, sure there was a market for the "carpet of the twenty-first century."

There were other problems with Bradfield's idea. The new backing would compete directly with Shaw's existing—and profitable—PVC-based carpet backing called Permabac. Since PVC plastic was the industry standard, Shaw would be bucking conventional carpet wisdom. Bradfield also proposed to locate his skunk works in the back of Shaw's new 1-million-square-foot manufacturing plant. This modern facility had been specially built a few years earlier to produce the highest-quality PVC backing in the industry—the very product Bradfield was planning to make obsolete. According to Bradfield, "It was a brand new plant that was not broken, and we asked them to fix it."[18]

In many companies, Bradfield's suggestion would have led to early retirement. But Shaw had a history of encouraging innovation and prudent risk taking. Bradfield got his money, his backroom skunk works, and even some encouragement from his superiors. Over the ensuing months, Bradfield and his team experimented with formulations, designs, and processes. Their work bore fruit. By 1999, they successfully produced a new carpet backing that met all the standard customer expectations for price, performance, and aesthetics, with the added advantage that it could provide the foundation for a new carpet that could potentially become the most completely recycled flooring on the market.

Shaw branded its new backing, EcoWorx, and launched it in 1999 in direct competition with the company's existing Permabac PVC-based backing. To the surprise of even the project champions, EcoWorx squeezed its PVC sibling entirely out of the marketplace within a few years. The speed of displacement was shocking. According to Bradfield, "We had no idea that we could phase out of PVC that quickly. Once we realized that customers were choosing EcoWorx over the PVC backing, we decided that the only way to make this truly successful was to mainstream it."[19] In a December 8, 2004, press release, Shaw announced the end of Permabac and the beginning of a new era for the company. In addition to a warm embrace from the marketplace, EcoWorx received the Environmental Protection Agency's 2003 "Designing Greener Chemicals Award" in recognition of its groundbreaking contribution to sustainability. Shaw's sustainability triumph also coincided with an acquisition offer from Berkshire Hathaway.

With its innovations, Shaw has successfully implemented the first three biosphere rules. Its parsimonious materials pallet comprises just two materials: the EcoWorx backing material and face fiber made of Nylon 6. It developed an energy-efficient system to recover its end-of-use tiles, separate the backing and face fiber, and pass each though its own cycling processes. The EcoWorx process was developed in-house. For the nylon process, Shaw purchased Evergreen, a carpet-recycling facility analogous to Polyamid, which was built by Honeywell and DSM in Augusta, Georgia. (Evergreen had been shut down in 2001 for basically the same reasons as Polyamid and remained mothballed until Shaw acquired it in 2006.) What made Shaw think it could be successful with Evergreen, when others failed? Shaw's parsimonious materials design meant much greater control over the waste carpet stream. As more and more of Shaw's carpet comes flowing back from its customers' floors, the company could eliminate the chaotic mix of waste carpet that wrecked Polyamid and Evergreen. Shaw continues to pursue increasing power autonomy—the company is decreasing its energy consumption by 3 percent every year based on 2005 estimates—and expects to see improving profitability. It also projects that it will eventually prevent three hundred million pounds of waste carpet from ending up in landfills annually.[20]

Economic Enabler 1: Material Content

Getting the right *types* of materials into products is a huge undertaking. But it is also important make sure that the *quantity* of material is available to create and sustain an economically viable value cycle. Previously we saw how the proliferation of material types, from nylon to natural fibers, created a management nightmare for Polyamid. But even when it was able to separate out the valuable nylon fiber carpets from the carpets that used different materials, it ran into an additional problem. When doing their financial analysis, Polyamid engineers had calculated that the average European nylon carpet was made up of 45 percent nylon face fiber. In reality, the amount of nylon in each carpet was far less. The well-meaning carpet companies had been pursuing the dictates of eco-efficiency and creating more carpet with less nylon, thinning the face fiber down to 25 percent nylon. Often called "dematerialization," the reduction of material content in products was widely understood as a sustainability best practice. But in the context of a value cycle, it had unintended consequences. According to a Polyamid technical manager, "The content of nylon in European carpet is less than expected and decreases every year."[21] The problem became so bad that Polyamid began sourcing waste carpet from the United States, where there was still a market for plush rugs with 45 percent nylon fiber. Still it wasn't enough. The economics of shipping waste carpet across the Atlantic meant that Polyamid would never profitably reach its target capacity. The lack of valuable materials in European carpet made recycling uneconomical.

As the case illustrates, managers need to be careful with eco-efficiency. The strategy makes sense for a company operating within a value chain where there is no plan to recover products at the end of their useful life. It also makes sense in terms of energy use, which can never be recovered. But it can be absolutely counterproductive for companies that want to recover and reuse materials after customer use. Managers therefore need to be very clear about whether they are dematerializing or value cycling.

Another example of the constraints that dematerializing can place on value cycling can be found in the bottling industry. According to Coca-Cola's vice president for sustainability, the industry's strategy for "sustainable packaging" has emphasized "light weighting," which is basically dematerialization applied to drink containers, that is, making more bottles from less plastic.[22] That makes sense if you're going to throw the bottle away, but can be a problem when you want to begin value cycling the plastic in the bottles. With current technology, you can put only about 10 percent to 25 percent recycled content into light-weighted bottles before you begin to create performance problems. However, if you make a slightly heavier package, you can quickly move to 50 percent or more recycled content. However, the light-weighting mind-set means that a slightly heavier product is perceived as backsliding on sustainability progress.

Ironically, you may need more content to create less waste via a value cycle. This is not a surprise to ecologists, of course. In nature, bacteria will recycle the carcass of a dead animal for the energy value left in it. If nature "eco-efficiencied" all the value from dead animals, the biosphere would collapse. Managers likewise need to consider the end-of-life value of their "commercially dead" products. The best way to do this is to begin thinking about the products in the hands of your customers as a resource deposit that the company will mine at a future date. In a copper mine, for example, if the percentage of valuable ore gets too low, operation of the mine becomes uneconomical. The same is true for value cycling. Those who want profitable end-of-life recycling have to ensure that there is a valuable stash of materials waiting.

Economic Enabler 2: Material Accessibility

Another problem that can doom value cycling efforts is the added costs of collecting and sorting through the tangled mess of materials in the product. While systematically pursuing materials parsimony can simplify this mess, designers can still render the valuable material nuggets irretrievable by gluing, encapsulating, bonding, or fusing them with other low-value or contaminating materials. Options for cycling materials in these conditions are limited to what can be called "grind and sort" approaches. In a grind-and-sort situation, products are passed through heavy equipment that pulverizes the recovered products and sends them to sifting machines that screen out metals and other valuable materials. The leftover waste is often sent to the landfill or, in the best cases, becomes filler or some other low-value additive. While grind-and-sort can capture some value, it is a distant second to true value cycling in terms of economic value to a company and of sustainability. The value that went into the product evaporates when grinding begins and the structure and design are pulverized. In contrast, products designed with materials accessibility in mind can offer up much more of their value than a few ounces of precious metals.

To illustrate the importance of materials accessibility for its clients, the consultancy MBDC organizes workshops in which senior managers tear down their own products using nothing but a basic set of hand tools. The results are often surprising and disturbing. In one case, it took three hours to disassemble a chair into its individual component parts, some of which could not be fully dismantled with the tools at hand. The lesson is obvious. Recovery requirements and economics have to be designed in from the start. MBDC, for example, recommended a product redesign so that the connections holding two parts together could be undone by one person in thirty seconds or less.

The international office furniture giant Steelcase has embodied this approach in its Think office chair. Working with MBDC, Steelcase selected a nontoxic parsimonious palette for the chair composed of a mere eight materials.[23] By weight, 99 percent of the materials are recyclable with existing processes. To make those materials quickly accessible, the chair is designed to come apart easily with simple hand tools. In fact, almost anyone can break the chair down into its constituent parts in about five minutes. None of the components are glued or encapsulated, and all parts weighing fifty grams or more are labeled for easy identification and recycling.

Implementing these design changes is not difficult, as long as it comes at the beginning of the new product development process. The changes often require only that the company establish a set of design guidelines and build awareness among product developers, designers, and engineers about end-of-life reuse and recycling needs. Hewlett-Packard, for instance, has created "Design for Recycling Rules" for engineers, which offers a simple checklist. The rules include things like no adhesives, more use of snap fittings, and clearly marking materials.[24] Many companies find these design improvements help in ways that extend beyond disassembly; they can also make assembly faster and more efficient, saving money at multiple points in the product's life cycle. The simplification of the Steelcase Think chair, for example, allows a five-minute breakdown that equally facilitates quick assembly. Siemens was able to reduce the number of parts in one of its personal computers from eighty-seven to twenty-nine, cutting the disassembly time from eighteen minutes to four. But it also reduced the assembly time from thirty-three minutes to seven.[25] Value cycling can pay both coming and going.

Challenges to Value Cycling

Companies employing a parsimonious materials palette capable of being recycled and easily accessed not only will want those materials back, but thcy will want them in good condition and ready for their next product incarnation. One of the biggest challenges in the back portion of the loop is thus specifying the quantity, quality, and usefulness of the incoming materials. Returned products and the materials they contain can vary in terms of cleanliness, wear, condition, location, and other factors. Rough handling or other abuse of products, whether during customer use or in the reverse logistics loop, create lots of variability. All this generates unpredictability and uncertainty that can doom the economics of the back-end of a value cycle. A big part of developing the value cycle is therefore creating a strategy to control variability and uncertainty.

Ideally, it would be great if products could talk, letting their makers know how they have been used and what condition they are in when they arrive at the recycling facility. Fuji Xerox's diagnostic tools allows all their products to "talk back," showing the power this can bring in performance management, but new information technologies and electronically enabled logistics can turbo-charge this vision. Sensors, data recorders, databases, and a whole host of other IT solutions can be applied to value cycle management. An easy first step is the use of simple barcodes that connect back to databases and keep records of where and when a product was sold and any maintenance or repairs done on it. But newer technologies can open even more transparent windows into a product's life experience. Robert Bosch Tool Corporation, for example, installs data collectors that capture information about usage in its power tools.[26] Embedded computer chips and technologies like radio frequency identification (RFID) tags can even provide real-time data about the state of the installed product base around the world.

Take the start-up iGPS as an example. The Florida-based company manufactures and deploys a pool of advanced plastic pallets used for logistics around the world. The pallets are fitted with RFID tags (the "i" in iGPS stands for intelligent) that allow the company to monitor their installed base of pallets traversing the globe. The retrieved information is invaluable to the iGPS, but also to their customers who can monitor the location and progress of their shipments. The use of the information system for value cycling is basically a collateral benefit. When one of the pallet breaks or fails, iGPS knows and can recover it for cycling back into the next generation of pallets.

Combining usage data like this with self-diagnostic technologies can help identify where problems lie, even before they cause a product failure. In effect, the technology allows products to report on how customers treat and use them. This can obviously raise some touchy privacy issues, so care is needed. And not all products require highly detailed information. The key is determining what information is required to ensure smooth and cost-effective value cycle operation and then developing an appropriate strategy to obtain it.

While having greater control over the condition in which products are returned is a big advance, it's not enough. Companies also need greater control over the timing of the product return. Ideally, manufacturers would like customers to upgrade to the next generation of products at a time that suits the value cycle. This may require "push" marketing efforts that invite customers to upgrade or provide incentives for repurchase. This means the end of the "sell it and forget it" relationship where products are out of mind once the first transaction takes place and a move to a "sell it, monitor it, recover it, cycle it, and sell it again" relationship. It puts a big twist on the old adage, "stay close to your customer."

The greatest challenge to the success of a value cycle will be cultural, however. In particular, sales, marketing, and accounting may have a difficult time adjusting to the new requirements of value cycle thinking. A very different set of marketing and sales skills are required to move inventory out the door than are needed to promote a product that you ultimately want to see again. It is the difference between executing a transaction and forging a relationship. The shift will require some wholesale changes in business models that will be discussed in detail in rule 5.

Nonetheless, some companies will resist making these investments at all. Partnerships and outsourcing relationships can and will evolve to deal with the companies that find themselves in the latter camp, and manufacturers will have to become adept at negotiating these relationships to protect their brand and interests. Managing these relationships to maximize value cycle performance and economics are discussed in the next chapter.

Making the Transition

For the foreseeable future, companies that have developed deep-loop value cycles will need to both source virgin materials and use recycled materials as input for their products. The percentage of materials that will come from recycled goods can increase over time and displace virgin input and as value cycles grow, and there is no reason that different companies can't use similar resources. In fact, Shaw is currently processing its competitor's carpet in its Evergreen facility, and there is nothing keeping Shaw from using nylon it recovers for something other than carpet. With a value cycle in place, companies have the potential to extend the value cycle strategies they develop for one product across any number of products.

That's the topic of the next chapter and rule 4 of the biosphere: platform leverage.

4

Sustainable Product Platforms

RULE 4

Leverage your value cycle as a product platform for scale,
scope, and knowledge economies.

There is more to be gained by producing more
opportunities than by optimizing existing ones.
—Kevin Kelley[1]

Building an economically viable value cycle, founded on a nontoxic, parsimonious materials pallet and energy-efficient process
technologies, is a big achievement. Some companies may be
satisfied to stop there, but that would be a mistake. Even greater
gains can be had by leveraging the company's value cycle as a

platform for creating new products and attacking fresh markets. This is where the returns from sustainability are amplified and durable competitive advantage is built (see table 4-1). I've focused on the surprisingly large and rapid gains that can come from turning value chains into value cycles. Pioneering companies have shown that building value cycles is a wise business investment. But while the return on investment is there, the amount of time, personnel, and capital required is not trivial. To maximize the return on these investments, early builders of value cycles can pursue the next biosphere rule by exploiting the latent economies of scale, scope, and knowledge inherent in a well-designed platform.

Fortunately, platform thinking is not new to business. It is a strategy that has been successfully exploited in a variety of industries, from automobiles to appliances, where a family of products shares similar components and parts. Platforms can take many forms, from proprietary to fully open-source. How to structure and design a value cycle platform and how to deal with ownership issues and incorporate business partners into new processes are important strategic considerations. Matching the right structure to the context will determine how well companies can leverage the

TABLE 4-1

The business benefits of increasing product platforms

Biosphere rule	Business benefit
Increasing product platforms	Compound above benefits through scale
	Compound above benefits through scope
	Foundation to accumulate learning by doing
	Build robust cross-industry platform demand

economies of scale, scope, and knowledge. The goal of building a sustainable product platform is not only to share physical assets among products but to embed learning, knowledge creation, and sustainability into the business across functional and, in some cases, organizational boundaries.

Nature's Way, Business's Way

Life shares a common, underlying design established by the earliest multicelled organisms more than three billion years ago. This life design has been exploited by the biosphere as a flexible foundation, a fundamental platform on which to build the Earth's thirty million or so different creatures. The term *platform* can have a variety of meanings in different settings. In theater, a platform is a stage, a foundation on which playwrights and actors create an endless variety of imaginary worlds, from Macbeth's Scottish castle to Godot's bench. In information technology, a platform is a foundational operating system, like Windows or UNIX, on which a limitless number of applications, from Acrobat to Excel, can be run. In nature, a platform is the combination of standardized elemental materials—the CHON described in rule 1—and a common set of solar-powered cyclical processes that transform raw materials into an astonishing variety of diverse organisms. It is an evolution-enabled system that conserves materials, but creatively destroys individual species in a process of constant, albeit gradual, innovation and change.

Today, nature's materials-process platform has been leveraged to create the incredible variety of organisms that fill every possible environmental niche. The platform's ability to extend to the planet's farthest reaches comes from its skill in generating increasing returns to scale, which are the key to self-sustaining growth. Stanford University economist Brian Arthur defines increasing returns as "the tendency for that which is ahead to get further ahead, for that which loses advantage to further lose advantage."[2] Common sayings capture the essence more simply: "Stick with a winner." "It takes money to make money." Increasing returns are the proverbial snowball effect in which growth is sustained through continuous compounding. While most managers think of increasing returns in terms of economies of scale, increasing returns in nature are more multifaceted than that. Nature's increasing returns are possible because of the biosphere platform's ability to simultaneously exploit economies of scale, scope, and knowledge.

Scale economies in the biosphere is primarily population growth; it is as nature's investment in the platform leveraged over the reproduction of a single species. Scope economies, on the other hand, can be seen in speciation, the evolutionary process of creating new and different species that are adapted to succeed in varying conditions—think of Darwin's finches. But more fundamentally, nature's platform makes use of knowledge economies through the encoding and sharing of survival information for each organism. As life evolves and adapts, it "learns" what works or doesn't through natural selection. This useful knowledge is conserved. The individual cells that make up our bodies, for example, essentially function identically with the cells of ancient planarians, and special learning accumulates and builds over time.

Nature's vehicle for encoding this information is DNA, which is retained at each evolutionary step and passed on to subsequent generations and species, expressing itself through function, form, and behavior. Evolutionary successes are committed to biochemical memory and passed on from generation to generation and along evolutionary chains. We've all heard that humans share more than 99 percent of our DNA with chimpanzees, and in doing so we exploit the accumulated wisdom of innumerable evolutionary experiments. Nature is constantly leveraging this know-how in ever-expanding knowledge economies.

The success of the biosphere's platform will come as no surprise to many executives. Platform strategies are also well known in business, where their historical role has been to leverage investments in design, materials, components, and processes across a growing output. Researchers Marc Meyer and Alvin Lehnard define a product platform as a "set of subsystems and interfaces that form a common structure from which a stream of derivative products can be efficiently developed and produced."[3] The automobile industry has long exploited just this kind of platform approach by using common subsystems like drive trains, engines, chassis, and other components. This allows carmakers to satisfy a variety of customer tastes from a common set of building blocks.

The strategy of leveraging a platform across models was a factor in the rise of General Motors over its rival Ford Motor Company in the 1920s. Ford himself was no stranger to the benefits of leverage, but almost exclusively emphasized economies of scale. In 1908, Ford started a revolution by originating standardization-driven industrial-scale economies to produce the first Model T. Ford adopted an assembly line production model inspired by the Chicago Union Stock Yards, where slaughterhouse efficiency was used to butcher pigs. By using standard components identical for every car, Ford built an efficient process of having workers deal with the same part in the same way in the same amount of time, every time. This production platform was then massively leveraged over an increasing output of vehicles.

Ford's mass production platform worked brilliantly, and the scale of his output drove the price of a Model T down to the point where even Ford's assembly line employees could afford to buy one. And while his competitors squealed, Ford's decision to pay workers an unheard of $5 dollars a day helped the company sell fifteen million "Tin Lizzies." But Ford's relentless focus on standardization-driven scale economies left the customer no choice. Ford is infamous for saying that buyers could have any color they wanted as long as it was black. And it was here that General Motors found opportunity. Unlike Ford, which made just one car, GM was a holding company for a number of different brands, all targeted to different customer segments. Chevrolet, Pontiac, Oldsmobile, Buick, and Cadillac were all sold under the GM umbrella by the early 1920s.

GM recognized the benefits of Ford's scale economies but found a way to exploit not just scale economies, but also scope economies, across its different brands. By leveraging common components across different cars, GM built a product platform that could produce cost-effective changes in design and style, allowing it to appeal to different customer segments. GM further leveraged its growing knowledge of the car market and customer needs to identify and build new product niches, from sedans and sports cars to station wagons and pickups. This scope economy approach permitted GM to maximize the use of its fixed-capital assets, materials, and processes across multiple brands in multiple product segments. The strategy drove profits up and allowed it to surpass Ford as the world's leading car manufacturer.

The platform tradition continues in the auto industry today with companies like Volkswagen claiming $1.7 billion a year in savings from leveraging its product platform across car lines.[4] VW products share exhaust systems, axles, brakes, and other components among four different brands: Audi, Volkswagen, Seat, and Skoda. Each brand is positioned for distinct market segments. The future of automobiles portends even more flexible platforms. In 2002, for example, GM unveiled a concept platform known as the Hy-Wire concept car. Powered by a hydrogen fuel cell, the design eliminates the engine block, steering wheel, drive train, and other mechanical linkages in favor of an all-electronic drive-by-wire system. What is left is literally a platform, a flat skateboard configuration on which GM can build a sport sedan, a minivan, or even a delivery truck.[5] The platform is extremely flexible and allows innumerable configuration innovations like altering the driver's location or the flexibility for owners to switch between passenger car and transport vehicle as needed. Whether or not the Hy-Wire enters into production, it points to the potential of future platform innovations.[6]

GM's Hy-Wire demonstrates how much has been learned about product platforms since the Model T. Companies across industries now employ mass customization and flexible manufacturing strategies in product platform and product family settings. These approaches succeed largely because they facilitate *simultaneous* economies of scope and scale. In effect, companies have learned to do in an industrial setting through platform development what nature has been doing in its biological setting for millennia.

Rule 4: Sustainable Product Platforms

Businesses can exploit nature's platform approach and generate increasing returns through the use of a sustainable product platform. A sustainable product platform is the combination of a parsimonious materials palette and associated processing technologies assembled into an economically viable value cycle that is flexible enough to produce a variety of products. If managers only used this combination for a single product, the increasing returns they could realize would come predominantly from scale economies, that is, spreading the fixed costs over an increasing unit output. But by treating the materials-process combination as a fundamental design platform and leveraging it across an entire family of products, managers can foster the scale, scope, and knowledge economies that will continually optimize the value cycle and build larger and more durable profits from their initial investment. How the platform is structured, in terms of who owns and controls the various platform elements and technologies, has an impact on a company's abilities to capture learning and knowledge economies and is therefore an important strategic question.

Sustainable Product Platforms in Practice

We can return to Shaw Industries for an example of how a company can leverage a sustainable product platform. Platforms like Shaw's build on our understanding of platform strategies, but go beyond the parts, components, and interfaces to the deeper materials and materials processing level.

In the previous chapter, we looked at how Shaw combined a parsimonious materials palette and energy-efficient process technologies to create a value cycle for the production and reprocessing of its carpet tiles. Shaw could have stopped there and limited the application to its commercial carpet tile business. Assuming it could capture growing market share, the company would experience scale economies as it expanded production of carpet tile. Cost reductions would come as Shaw recovered nearly cost-free waste carpet tiles and used them as raw material production inputs. It would also save on processing costs because its value cycle was more efficient than virgin production. But stopping there would miss out on opportunities to leverage the materials and value cycle process in other market segments.

Commercial carpet tiles, while an important segment, account for only 47 percent of the carpet market. Residential broadloom, the rolled-style carpet used in people's homes, accounts for 53 percent of the market. In 2006, Shaw announced a new product line, EcoWorx Performance Broadloom. By doing so, the company leveraged its platform investment from office spaces into residential carpeting. The opportunity was created by focusing innovation efforts on a search for ways to apply the EcoWorx technology platform to new markets. The commercial tile business didn't go away, of course. Instead, with this extension, Shaw could substantially increase the scale and scope of production, leveraging its platform assets to new markets. The power of this approach is not just that it provides additional returns on Shaw's original investment in developing EcoWorx or that it opens new markets for Shaw. By leveraging its platform, Shaw substantially strengthened its value cycle by creating a more diverse, robust, and predictable supply of end-of-life inputs for the future.

Another example of a sustainable platform can be found in the consumer products industry. In 2006, Oakland, California–based Clorox Company made an important foray into the world of sustainable product platforms with the introduction of the

Green Works line of cleaners. The project began as a skunk-works initiative pursued by a handful of environmentally conscious researchers in the Clorox Technology Center, where new products are developed and tested. When Clorox managers identified sustainability as an important and lasting market trend, the researchers were given the green light to develop their idea for eco-friendly cleaning products.[7] Clorox chose to make cleaners out of entirely natural ingredients, that is, ingredients derived solely from natural sources like plants. In effect, Clorox was choosing to tap into nature's value cycle for its inputs and recycling, something that makes sense for a product like a glass cleaner, which is completely dispersed by use, leaving nothing left over for Clorox to take back as an input. Developing a materials palette entirely of natural ingredients that worked as well as existing products like Clorox's Formula 409 cleaner was no easy feat. According to Clorox's vice president for sustainability, Bill Morrissey, the launch of Green Works was delayed several times because the company was determined to get the products right.[8] When it finally launched the first five products under the Green Works brand, the customer response exceeded the team's wildest expectations. Clorox had a winner. Almost overnight, Clorox became the leader in the natural cleaning products category, dwarfing long-term eco-companies like Seventh Generation and method.

Clorox's natural product platform was helping to build market share in its existing segments, but could it help the company expand into new territory? A $5 billion company, Clorox is a relatively small player compared to industry titans like Procter & Gamble and Unilever. Challenging these marketing powerhouses with "me too" products would be a dubious proposition. But could the Green Works platform provide new opportunities for competitive strategy? In 2008, Clorox released the new Green Works Natural Dishwashing Liquid, its first-ever foray into dish soap, going head to head with the category leaders. According to a Green Works manager the results are encouraging; market research indicates that the Green Works dish soap was substantially outselling competitors' offerings.[9] Successes like this have reinforced Clorox's commitment to making sustainability a core pillar of its future growth strategy. Expect to see additional products building off the Green Works platform in new segments and sectors.

Another example can be found at Recycline, an environmentally conscious plastics recycler established in the mid-1990s. Company founder Eric Hudson developed his first product in 1996. The Preserve Toothbrush is made from recovered plastic waste and sells in retail outlets like Trader Joe's supermarkets. Preserve's success drew the attention of environmentally minded companies, and in 2000, Hudson was approached by eco-leader Stonyfield Farm about collaborating to recycle Stonyfield's waste polypropylene plastic yogurt cups. The partnership has proved successful and has supported the growth of Recycline's platform beyond toothbrushes. Today, Recycline produces a growing line of personal care products including razors and tongue cleaners, as well as broad array of tableware and kitchen products. Each new product leverages Recylcine's platform, adding to the sales and growth of the company.

Platform Design

As the previous examples illustrate, the purpose of platform approaches is to design, engineer, and exploit commonalities among different products, processes, and markets, while simultaneously addressing variety in market demand and lowering costs. Naturally, this has important implications for company operations, from both tactical and strategic perspectives. On the tactical side, platform thinking must be integrated into the design guidelines and engineering criteria for existing and new products. These criteria will also influence supplier and customer relationships. On the strategic side, managers will need to identify the best way to structure their platform, clarifying which elements should be kept within the organization and which can be outsourced to partners. However, because all elements of the platform must function as part of an integrated value cycle and not a linear "sell it and forget it" value chain, it demands greater coordination, information exchange, and mutual learning.

Platform design therefore needs to focus on how to organizationally structure, manage, and execute platform tasks. The success of these decisions in turn determines how effectively a company can exploit increasing return economies and appropriate the collateral benefits. This is important because increasing returns drive platform profitability and thus financial sustainability of the effort.

The scale and scope economies already discussed are relatively straightforward, but knowledge economies require additional consideration. Knowledge economies are driven by how well a company captures useful information produced at different points in the value cycle and then utilizes the information to drive constant improvements in overall value cycle function. All the processes in the value cycle—production, customer use, disassembly, reprocessing, and so on—will throw off valuable information that can be used to refine and optimize the overall platform function. Different platform design choices, such as vertical integration versus process outsourcing, will influence how well knowledge economies are captured and utilized. Effective platform strategies will therefore need to explicitly consider knowledge economies at the outset and build in management systems to ensure their optimal exploitation.

Platform Tactics

Companies should be guided in their platform tactics by the type of value cycle they are pursuing—deep-loop, shallow-loop, or both. In a deep-loop value cycle, such as the ones developed by Recycline, Clorox, and Shaw, the commonality shared by the involved products is the materials and processing technologies used to manufacture them. When the deep-loop value cycle developed for one product is used as a platform, it is fundamentally leveraging the materials palette and processes across different products within a company's family of brands and lines. The principal tactics that make this possible occur in the product design and development phase when managers decide what the product will be made of and how it will be produced.

It may seem counterintuitive, but the primary way to foster platform innovation is to constrain the design discretion given to development teams when they are designing new products. In effect, designers and engineers need to stop asking, "What materials can I use for this product?" and start asking, "How can I design this product with my existing materials palette and processing technologies?" As mentioned, many managers recoil at the idea of constraining design discretion, seeing it as a limitation on innovation. But as nature's creativity demonstrates, constraining material choices has not inhibited the innovative power of the biosphere.

The truth is that all innovation is subject to constraints, the most basic being the laws of physics. Society also depends on constraints, the most basic of which is a common language. Constraints are needed to ensure that the system, be it communication or computation, functions as an efficient whole. Similarly, in order to create an efficient sustainable product platform, all the elements must conform to the needs of the overall system. As Todd Copeland, a materials and environmental manager at outdoor equipment maker Patagonia told me, "In order to make a recyclable product, we have to design it to meet the criteria of the recycling system. Design and manufacturing become linked into all of your business decisions and need to feed into planning and strategy."[10]

Innovating under sustainability constraints is part of the change in thinking that occurs as a company moves from value chain to value cycle to sustainable platform thinking. With value chain thinking, a product is viewed as a separate and independent artifact that can be optimized in isolation. But with a value cycle, and especially as part of a platform, the product becomes one element in a larger system that lives on, even after the artifact's usefulness has passed. In this sense, products are a temporary configuration of a company's platform assets put into the service of a customer's current needs. It's a very different way of thinking about products.

This can be a big shift in mind-set for design teams, but the results can be innovative and interesting. When Herman Miller engineers were informed that the company's Design for Environment system had rejected, for recyclability reasons, the spine design for the new Mirra desk chair, they initially grumbled at the imposition. But they went back to the drawing board. The resulting redesign created breakthroughs that saved money, increased performance, and resulted in a new patentable innovation.[11] These types of redesign innovations can foster ingenious advances, like making materials useful in places once thought impossible. Aluminum, for example, has long been sought for automobile and other applications, because its light weight translates into significant fuel savings, compared with steel. But aluminum is less rigid than steel and thus limited in the number of places it can be used. However, engineers have been able to extend the potential uses for aluminum through a creative design change that uses a honeycomb system to strengthen the metal. This allows it to be integrated into previously impossible applications.

Of course, some designers will resist the constraints, but innovative companies recognize that constraints can drive innovation. Janine Benyus, one of the leading thinkers on the practice known as biomimicry in which innovators use nature as an inspiration for human technology, claims that nature's success comes from tapping into the power of limits and using it to foster novelty.[12] Amazon.com founder Jeff Bezos echoed this sentiment, "Frugality drives innovation, just like other constraints do. One of the only ways to get out of a tight box is to invent your way out."[13] Support for the innovative power of limits can also be found among academics. Harvard Business School guru Michael Porter, for example, argued in a 1995 *Harvard Business Review* article that countries that constrain environmentally damaging business practices through proactive regulatory constraints promote greater innovation and dynamism in their economies.[14] Thus, one of the first and most important tactics in leveraging a deep-loop value cycle into a platform is well-thought-out design constraints on new product development teams, asking them to design not just for the product but also for the platform.

Enforcing materials commonality is the primary tactic companies pursuing deep-loop platform leverage will use, but for many companies, shallow-loop cycling suggests other opportunities. In these cases, commonality doesn't stop at the materials level but can be extended upward to components and parts, as is common in more traditional product platform strategies. In order for product platforms to function, components need to be modular and share common "plug-and-play" connections.

Platform Ownership

The tactic of constraining design flexibility in the interest of fostering platform commonality facilitates the extension of the basic materials and processes over a growing volume of products in deep-loop strategies, while common components foster shallow-loop applications. But while designing products to fit into a platform model is an enabling step, there are important strategic decisions executives need to make about how the platform itself will be structured and managed organizationally.

As shown in figure 4-1, platform designs can reside along a spectrum going from full vertical integration to completely open-sourced. Initially, however, most companies will strategically manage platforms in one of two ways, either through vertical integration or a partnership approach. The appropriate option depends on the resources, assets, and capabilities of individual companies, as well as the nature of the product and industry in which companies compete. Each approach has its virtues and challenges.

As managers contemplate how to design their platform, many will find that there are existing recycling infrastructures operating in their industries. Most of the recycling we see today

FIGURE 4-1

Platform governance spectrum

There are a variety of ways a platform can be designed and managed. Choosing the right mix of capabilities and control is vital to achieving economies of scale, scope, and knowledge.

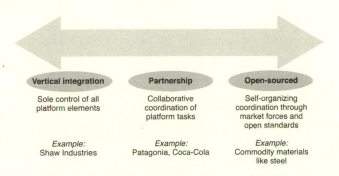

is not managed by the original equipment manufacturer (OEM) that designed and manufactured the product. Instead, product recovery and recycling has developed informally, often by opportunistic third parties that find ways to extract residual value from end-of-life products. The biosphere metaphor for this type of activity is "scavenging," which is an important ecological function in most ecosystems. Scavengers recover dead creatures and extract any remaining nutritional and energy value from the carcass. In many sectors like paper, metal, and plastic recycling, scavenging has helped recover and reuse valuable materials that would otherwise end up in landfills. However, as companies implement the biosphere rules, some may find they need to strategically rethink this approach.

Since the earliest days of the car industry, for example, independent junkyards and shredders pulled usable parts from cars and recycled the steel and other valuable metals from automobile hulks. Auto recyclers can be quite efficient with valuable materials: more than 90 percent of car steel is recycled, for example. In contrast, the plastic and other nonmetal components of the car tend to end up as shredder waste and can account for 25 percent of the total waste materials volume.[15] As car manufacturers have shifted to more plastics, the percentage of shredder waste is growing. This waste exists because cars historically have not been designed with a value cycle in mind.

Scavenging in this fashion can be financially expedient but also poses concerns for some companies. In the electronics industry, for example, recycling effort focuses on extracting the small quantities of precious materials that reside in waste products. The U.S. Geological Survey estimates that for every one million cell phones disposed of, four tons of gold could be recovered.[16] But in most cases, recovering the precious metals is labor intensive, which can make recovery uneconomical in high-wage labor markets. Because of this, computers, monitors, printers, and keyboards that have been collected for recycling in the United States are often packed into containers and shipped to low-cost labor countries in Asia and Africa, where laborers break them down by hand and extract the residual copper and minute amounts of gold or printer carbon ink. The recycling processes used in these countries are often hazardous and done in primitive conditions that expose the laborers to toxic fumes, lead, dioxins, and other poisons. The worthless hulks of leftover plastic casings are then dumped unceremoniously into river beds or along the side of the road.

In addition to the ethics of the situation and the potential liability issues, scavenging like this can present important risks to an OEM's brand and reputation. The ubiquity of the Internet means few places in the world are "out of sight," and a company that allows its products to be exported risks a YouTube video showing poor workers breaking down its products in hazardous conditions. When *Life* magazine published photographs of child laborers sewing Nike soccer balls in Pakistan, it caused an international scandal that forced the sporting goods company to completely rethink its sourcing practices.

In addition to risks to reputation, some companies have also become concerned about third parties sourcing and reselling their components. OEMs usually have no connections with and no control or influence over the scavenging companies and therefore no way to stop others from recovering and remarketing their branded products or components. The risk is that parts or products that fail to meet the OEM's quality, performance, or aesthetic standards end up in the marketplace and cause damage to the brand and to the OEM's reputation. Furthermore, scavenging could also involve the involuntary transfer of design know-how and intellectual property. In many cases, disassembly requires a recycler to reverse engineer a product in order to break it down without damaging components or valuable elements. This can expose the intellectual property and design expertise in a product to third parties. The more expert a third party gets at breaking down and rebuilding a company's product, the greater the risk that important competitive advantages leak out and degrade.

In recognition of these issues, some companies have begun to forward-integrate their supply chains into the end-of-life stage for brand and reputational reasons only. The carmakers BMW, Ford, and Mercedes-Benz have at times purchased junkyards to gain more control over their end-of-life products and capture the profits realized by the third-party remanufacturers.[17] This phenomenon is not limited to the automobile industry. A leading manufacturer of office furniture moved into refurbishing its own products because intermediaries were selling second-hand cubicles, desks, and chairs with the company's brand name still on them. This situation becomes even more problematic when the company's profitability depends on refills and resupplying equipment to current customers.

Printer maker Lexmark, for example, confronted this issue when third-party companies began recovering and refilling its printer cartridges at a substantial discount. Besides the lost market share, Lexmark worried that its brand name could be damaged by low-quality refills that resulted in bad printing. To regain control, in 1997, Lexmark created the "prebate" program for its Optra S printer cartridges. The program gives customers an upfront discount in exchange for an agreement to return used cartridges for refill only to Lexmark. By prebating, Lexmark prevents customers from selling cartridges to third-party refillers, which are part of a $60 million dollar industry made up of thousands of small businesses. As one might expect, the reactions to Lexmark's actions were not universally positive. Consumer advocates and refillers made the program the target of legal complaints, claiming Lexmark is unfairly targeting the printer-cartridge remanufacturing business. Refillers scored a victory when the North Carolina legislature outlawed the practice in the state. Regardless of whether Lexmark or the refillers prevail, other manufacturers are already considering similar policies. Competitors HP and Samsung have even set up printer fraud squads of CSI-like detectives charged with nabbing cartridge counterfeiters.[18]

The business motivation for these companies is easy to understand. But there is a broader lesson for those that invest in building sustainable product platforms, as the case of Alberto Sanchez illustrates. An entrepreneur in Costa Rica, Sanchez has made an unlikely career of building value cycles in the country's agricultural sector.[19] One of his first efforts was a project initiated to address a pressing waste problem: chicken poop. The accumulation of chicken waste was becoming a political issue in Costa Rica, and the poultry industry was searching for a solution. In response, Sanchez created a process to convert poultry waste into organic fertilizer. While it sounds simple, developing an efficient system that met public health codes and customer demands was a substantial undertaking. To make his investment pay off, Sanchez needed a reliable supply of raw material input, so he negotiated a favorable five-year deal with the largest poultry companies. His product, branded Biofert, became a success.

A little over four years into the business, however, Sanchez was approached by the poultry producers who were supplying Biofert's chicken-waste input. Instead of thanking him for taking the waste problem off their hands, they instead wanted to buy him out. They presented Sanchez with a take it or leave it deal. Either he could sell them his business or say goodbye to the flow of fresh chicken waste. What could he do? Without a supply of waste, Sanchez's production facility was worthless. He was thus forced to sell to the poultry producers, who then vertically integrated their operations to include the business of organic fertilizer production.

Out of business, Sanchez began thinking about closing other product cycles in the agricultural sector.[20] He turned his attention to the citrus industry, where Costa Rican juice producers had their own waste problem: orange rinds. The large accumulating piles of orange waste were causing public health and nuisance problems for the juice companies as they rotted slowly in open dumps. Sanchez again used his entrepreneurial drive and built a business that consisted of buying up orange waste and converting it into fertilizer. But in a case of déjà vu, within a short period of time, he was approached by orange growers who wanted to buy him out and was again forced to sell the business. Sanchez is currently working on a new waste venture. This time perhaps he'll earn the title of entre-manure.

But the lesson of Sanchez's experiences is that once waste is recognized as valuable input, there is a potent incentive for the producer of that waste to retain ownership. This is a key insight for companies pursuing sustainable product platform strategies, because the very act of creating a parsimonious materials palette and an economic value cycle means waste becomes valuable input. If it's true for chicken poop, imagine what it means for carefully designed products. Given this reality it should be no surprise that competition for waste materials is already on the rise. In July 2008, National Public Radio reported that organized gangs had begun to raid San Francisco's recycling bins, stealing the valuable metals and other wastes.[21]

Vertically Integrated Platforms

Since the ascendance of the business doctrine of core competency, many companies have deintegrated, spinning off or selling parts of their supply chains and distribution. It might seem anathema to consider reintegration, particularly vertical integration, to include what we currently think of as waste. Vertical integration of the value cycle can be a high-cost approach, but it can also offer commensurate advantages. For first movers particularly, it may be the best way to foster ongoing differentiation and competitive advantage via the product platform. This is because a product platform isn't just about integrating materials into a closed-loop process. It is also about integrating business functions, including product design, manufacturing, sales, service, recovery, reuse, and recycling into a continuous whole. Doing so exploits economies of knowledge and learning that can create valuable and differentiating core competencies.

The power of this integration comes from sharing information and feedback that improves both individual operations and the overall function of the entire value cycle. This is the "knowledge economies" benefit of platforms discussed at the beginning of the chapter. In the biosphere, knowledge economies work through Darwinian survival of the fittest, in which effective survival mechanisms are captured and passed to subsequent generations and future species through DNA. Biologists refer to genetic features that are "highly conserved," meaning the same process is used in vastly different species. Information gathered through recovery and recycling efforts can work the same way. It can be fed back into product design and manufacturing to improve the efficiency and effectiveness of the value cycle.

This is not as easy as it sounds. Sharing information between functions within an organization can be a challenge. Even once the information is shared, getting designers to actually apply it is another issue, especially in environments where a "not invented here" mentality prevails. This is one of the reasons vertical integration can be a strategically attractive platform-design option. Information sharing inside an organization is usually easier than sharing useful know-how with other businesses, even when they are called "partners." Because building a sustainable product platform is an innovation initiative, learning quickly from mistakes and successes is important. Although sharing information among partnering organizations is possible, it is likely to be less efficient than sharing within an organization.

The added costs of vertical integration are balanced by the learning gains. Take the disassembly step in a value cycle. The entity doing the disassembly gains important knowledge about the state of the product, its potential cause of failure, and how the customer used it, among a host of other insights. This information is invaluable to the producer because it can use it to improve the overall performance and functionality of the product for the customer. It can also foster innovations that improve manufacturing or lower costs. Fuji Xerox, for example, found through the remanufacture of printer components that adding a simple coil spring would double the life of one part that was often failing. This simple redesign saved the company $40 million.[22]

In fact, when Fuji Xerox's Dan Godamunne talks about the company's approach, his vision goes well beyond component and materials flows. The intellectual and informational flow, like the genetic information cycled from generation to generation in nature, is cycled through the Fuji Xerox procreation, or product development, process. The company sees a value cycle that goes from the initial product concept all the way to end of life and tries to design all the system aspects in a continuous loop. According to Godamunne, "We get the maximum benefit, not just of the product itself, but also the technology, the research, and all the development activities in what we call a continuous feed system."[23] Godamunne aims to maximize the applicability of all the "brain power and money and investment" that go into developing innovative solutions across the organization's offerings. The discoveries and know-how are fed back to the new product development teams so they can be incorporated into the next generation of products, thus tapping into and exploiting the knowledge economies created by the value chain insights.

This feedback of know-how helps strengthen and improve the overall function of the platform. The knowledge gained in disassembly, for example, can improve performance at multiple stages of the value cycle. One European computer manufacturer found that the knowledge it gained from disassembly and fed back into product assembly cut fabrication costs by 50 percent.[24] Sony similarly found that in-house efforts to recover and recycle products enhanced product design and increased the percentage of recoverable and recyclable components in its computers.[25]

A vertically integrated platform is not the only way to generate and capture knowledge economies. Some may argue that within a well-structured and functional outsourcing relationship, this information will be transferred anyway. But disassembly and related know-how is frequently "tacit knowledge," meaning it can't be adequately captured in blueprints or manuals. It has to be transferred by one-on-one exchanges and direct experiences.

Some companies are developing the equivalent of corporate research laboratories to facilitate exchange of this knowledge. IBM, for example, operates an Asset Recovery Center, where it studies strategies for product disassembly and recovery and looks to improve the efficiency of its design efforts as they relate to value cycle management. BMW's German Recycling and Disassembly Center optimizes the time and tools needed to take apart used Beemers. The information also makes BMW's assembly processes more efficient. A formal, in-house center for the exchange of knowledge is not necessary for everyone. But given that most of the initial information needed for creating a profitable platform is tacit, it is ideally transferred through direct exchanges between people. Frequent exchanges between line employees, designers, engineers, marketing people, and senior management should thus be planned in implementing a sustainable product platform. Colocating disassembly and reassembly in the same facility, at least at the initial stages, can help foster information exchanges that improve overall functioning of the value cycle.

Platform Partnerships

An alternative to vertical integration is partnering and establishing concrete business links through collaborative agreements. The biospheric analog of this approach is symbiosis. Many companies will be attracted to or even dependent on partnerships in building a platform because they often don't control, or have the resources to develop, the processing technologies needed to close their value cycle. In this case, a symbiotic partnership is a good alternative. However, it requires building an association that goes beyond the traditional arm's-length transaction relationship because of the need to agree on the design constraints that ensure efficient functioning between value cycle handoffs.

An example of a company partnering to build a platform and then leveraging it across a growing number of products is the sports equipment and apparel retailer Patagonia. From roots going back to the early 1950s, Patagonia was founded in 1972 by Yvon Chouinard. The result of Chouinard's and his friends' love of the outdoors, the company was built with a strong environmental ethic. The company has a commitment to high-quality, long-lasting products, but also recognizes that no garment lasts forever. Given this, Patagonia has taken responsibility for its end-of-life products. According to Patagonia's environmental analysis director, Jill Dumain, the company began partnering early on with a company called Wellman, Inc. In the early 1990s Wellman started collecting recycled bottles and making polyester fiber for clothing. The bottles were shredded, melted, and reextruded as yarn to make soft fleece that would then go into

Patagonia jackets, vests, and pants. The process was limited and produced spun yarn that was appropriate for only a fraction of the Patagonia product line.[26]

Slick-surface clothing like shells and rain jackets require a high-performance filament that can be woven into polished fabric, something beyond the capabilities of the Polartec process. Patagonia wanted to do more. Instead of trying to find new vendors, Dumain says that the company would "work within our existing supply chain to find partners that are willing to change." Patagonia found just such a partner in Teijin, a Japan-based textile manufacturer. Teijin had developed a depolymerization process in the late 1990s that allowed it to convert wastes like bottles and shower curtains into a quality filament fiber perfectly suited to Patagonia's high-performance applications. Teijin had already collaborated with the Japanese government to create its Eco-Circle program that recovered uniforms from municipal workers and recycled the uniforms into fiber. Based on this promising potential, the two companies discussed the possibility of recycling Patagonia's used garments into new products.

It quickly became clear that success depended on moving beyond arm's-length supplier relations and into a long-term partnership. It was apparent to Patagonia that Teijin was not a mere recycler, but a sophisticated closed-loop fiber manufacturer. In fact, Teijin had made a large capital investment in the polyester-recycling process, so the partnership needed to ensure an attractive proposition for both parties. According to Dumain, Patagonia couldn't treat "our partner as a 'responsible garbage can' or as just a recycler."[27]

Instead, it would be creating a shared platform, which meant Patagonia had to make design changes to its clothing in order to produce a stream of waste fabric that would work well with the

Teijin processes. According to Patagonia manager Todd Copeland, "It was really a symbiotic relationship because they did a lot of mutual product development with us. Teijin's depolymerization process wasn't the hard part. The hard part was getting the garments into the right form to go through the chemical process."[28] This meant keeping low levels of contamination, that is, the amount of nonpolyester materials, which demanded a parsimonious materials palette. If Patagonia designs were made with a blend of polyester and other fibers like nylon, for example, the resulting material could gum up the Teijin process. The partners collaboratively established design constraints, such as controlling the variety of dyes and trim (zippers, buttons, and so on) to meet the needs of the emerging collaborative platform.

After substantial work to solve these problems, Patagonia launched the Common Threads Recycling Program in 2005 as a new closed-loop, clothing-to-clothing product platform. The inaugural product was Patagonia's Capilene brand of long underwear. When the underwear wears out, customers mail it back or bring it to the store so that Patagonia can cycle it into next season's garments. The process currently costs Patagonia more than virgin materials, due mostly to the preprocessing and trans-Pacific shipping. Patagonia has published a detailed study showing that the process creates a net environmental benefit by consuming 76 percent less energy than virgin processes, despite the long-distance transport. It's a good environmental story that resonates with Patagonia's customers and builds the eco-credibility of the Patagonia brand. The key to profitability, however, lies in expanding the scale and streamlining the process through refined designs and improved platform efficiencies.

Patagonia already is working on scaling, primarily by leveraging the Common Threads Recycling Program more broadly across its product line. In 2007, it expanded the offerings to include fleece garments and plans to continue adding products like running shorts and jackets as they are redesigned and new applications are found. As of the fall of 2009, 80 percent of Patagonia apparel was recyclable through the Common Threads program. The company aims to have all of its products be recyclable by the end of 2010 while acknowledging it doesn't know how it's going to meet the goal. Patagonia's statement about the products it is still struggling with serves as an object lesson in the importance of a parsimonious materials palette: "The most challenging clothing items yet to be recyclable are down-filled garments, shells with polyurethane barriers, fabrics with high spandex content, and small items that contain more trim than fabric—down insulation is reusable, but we have not found a way to successfully remove it from a shell; polyurethane barriers and spandex pose problems to both chemical and mechanical recycling processes; and small items are a challenge for sorting and removing trims."[29] While Patagonia is still working out how to recycle all its garments, it's also taking a page from Alberto Sanchez. The company has begun accepting any customers' polyester clothing, regardless of the manufacturer, as long as it is branded with the Polartec logo. In a press release, Patagonia's vice president of environmental initiatives said, "With the expansion of our Common Threads Recycling Program, we'll effectively be recycling our competitors' garments into Patagonia clothing . . . what a great, environmentally sensitive way to supply our own supply chain!"[30]

An alternative version of building a collaborative platform is found at Atlanta-based Coca-Cola Company. When most consumers think of Coke, they envision the classic glass bottle that has served as an iconic brand symbol for decades. Yet Coke today distributes almost 50 percent of its soda in plastic bottles.[31] These bottles are made out of polyethylene terephthalate, otherwise known by its acronym, PET. Coke had been exploring options for recycling its PET bottles for years, but felt that the technology to cost-effectively turn old bottles into new ones had not yet matured. Because recycling technology was beyond its core competency, Coke was counting on plastic recycling experts to develop the needed techniques.

One company working on the challenge was United Resource Recovery Corporation (URRC), which got its start by recovering the thin but valuable coating of silver found on used X-ray film collected from dentists and doctors.[32] The backing of an X-ray is made of PET, and URRC found that in the process of removing the silver, it was left with an incredibly clean sheet of plastic. Since PET was a desirable manufacturing material, URRC founder Carlos Gutierrez began looking for opportunities to recycle it for applications like soda bottles. Most existing PET recyclers for food packaging relied on a cleaning process akin to using soapy bubbles and hot water to scrub the plastic to FDA-approved "food grade" use. This approach, however, was energy intensive and costly. Gutierrez had alternatively developed a patented depolymerization process to chemically break down the PET, but it too was costly. In 1996, URRC found, however, that it could use the depolymerization process to remove only a thin outer layer of PET, much like peeling the brown layer off an onion. The process produced super-clean PET flakes that were ideal for food-grade uses. It also eliminated much of the energy and many of the steps found in other recycling approaches, steps that, according to URRC vice president Gerry Fishbeck, "add cost, require additional capital, and reduce the opportunity to create value."[33]

Coke began supporting URRC's efforts in 1996 and helped it demonstrate the commercial viability of the process. By 1998, the first licenses to use the technology were sold in Europe, Mexico, and Philippines. Coke hoped that private funding would be available to roll out the technology in the United States, and by early 2000, URRC was working with venture capitalists to secure the required funds. But the investment community turned out to be gun-shy, partly because some had been burned by failed recycling investments in the 1980s. This was frustrating; according to Fishbeck, "Coke said, 'No one seems to be picking up this ball for the high-end recycling of materials, but the world needs it.'"[34] By 2007, Coke decided it couldn't wait for the private investors and proposed a partnership with URRC to construct a U.S. facility.

In 2008, Coke and URRC announced they would collaboratively build the world's largest PET-recycling facility in Spartanburg, South Carolina. Opened in 2009, the plant uses patented URRC UnPET technology to clean recovered containers to food-grade quality and send it to Coke's North Carolina bottling plant for reprocessing into new bottles. The bottle-to-bottle recycling facility represents a deep-loop value cycle for Coke's product packaging. Establishing the platform, however, demanded a partnership that had developed over nearly a decade. By working together, the companies have created a platform that they hope will prove both ecologically and financially successful. According to Fishbeck, "The trick at the end of the day is simplifying the Spartanburg process to minimize the number of steps in getting the recycling done. That's how you eliminate costs and make the system more efficient."[35]

There are obvious benefits to using symbiotically driven partnerships for platform development. Each of the partners can focus on its core competencies and manage the portion of the value cycle it knows best. However, there are challenges to formal partnerships as well. Some, such as the risk of outsourcing disassembly, are the same as those in scavenging. Communication can also break down between partners, making knowledge and learning more difficult to share and delaying improvements to the cycle itself.

How Far Can Platforms Extend?

Most examples of sustainable product platform development are either those in which value cycle partners collaborate or companies integrate vertically. Many materials and processing technologies can find application in a wide range of products and industries, however. Nature spreads the benefits of a common platform and knowledge base across millions of species and regions. Likewise, the scale economies fostered by materials and product platforms can potentially extend beyond any individual company's product line. It is feasible that over time, materials platforms will expand and be broadly adopted by entire industries or sectors. The scale benefits of materials standards and shared product platforms could create industrywide or even economywide gains.

The Society for Organizational Learning (SoL), founded by MIT's Peter Senge, author of *The Fifth Discipline*, created the Materials Pooling Project, a concept originated by Michael Braungart, to explore the potential for shared material standards among industries. By suggesting that what any one company can do is limited, the project seeks to foster cross-sector collaboration.[36] In SoL meetings, member companies such as Harley-Davidson,

Nike, and Visteon Corporation have explored how a group of companies can pool demand and knowledge sharing around a common set of materials. The hope is that members can foster innovation, scale economies, and resultant cost savings. Thus they would collectively create a materials platform shared by different industries.

We can already see the outlines of these broader platforms in this chapter. Patagonia's and Coke's platforms share largely common materials. Like Patagonia, Coke has even gone so far as to create its own clothing line, which includes men's and women's T-shirts, tote bags, caps, purses, messenger bags, and notebooks, made from its recycled soda bottles. The line, branded "rPET," was originally offered only at the New World of Coca-Cola tourist attraction in Atlanta, Georgia. The fabrics were part of a "Drink 2 Wear" advertising campaign the company ran in television, radio, and print outlets in 2007 and 2008.

The clothing line is part of Coke's larger exploration of the challenges of building a viable value cycle. Thinking strategically, Coke's vice president for sustainability, Scott Vitters, says it helps to build local end markets for the needed materials to encourage a robust supply situation.[37] PET is a flexible product that can be used in fiber, clothes, upholstery, carpet, car components, strapping, and things like thermoform clam shells. But there is a challenge in encouraging a healthy materials market: it can potentially increase competition for waste materials. Coke is obviously not interested in running up prices and wants to capture and keep the waste bottles it collects. These competing needs—a healthy market versus controlling your own supply—make managing broader materials platforms a more complicated challenge.

Competitors' activities need to be taken into account. In Coke's case, many companies package their products—from drinks to dish soap—in PET containers. Some companies, however, increase demand for postconsumer PET by using it in their packages, but at the same time destroy supply by contaminating the plastic with color additives or by mixing contaminating materials in their containers. It is clear that broadly shared platforms need the same type of platform design constraints as vertically integrated or partnership approaches. Establishing needed standards is obviously more challenging to achieve in an open system.

Sustainable product platforms are still emerging, so it is difficult to know what the future of such ideas like materials pooling and open-source systems holds. It seems likely that different industries could use similar sustainable product platforms, based on a small number of materials and processes for many of their products. From this process, it is also likely that the materials best suited to value cycling will become apparent and global standards could emerge. Can a small number of sustainable product platforms colonize multiple industrial niches? The answer is in the hands of today's sustainable product platform pioneers.

In nature, a single basic platform is used to an incredible profusion. In this platform, there is no central manager organizing all aspects. It is a self-organizing system based on a simple set of standard rules. Inevitably, human industry will move toward a similar self-organizing system, guided by the invisible hand of market forces, constrained by a small set of standards.

5

Function over Form

RULE 5

Fulfill customers' functional needs in ways that
sustain the value cycle.

Own Nothing, Have Everything.
—Napster advertising slogan[1]

The idea of "servicization" or functional business models that deemphasize the product in favor of the functional benefit the product provides has been circulating for some time. The suggested benefits for companies usually include higher margins, more stable streams of revenue, and long-term relationships with customers (see table 5-1). Some companies have successfully implemented the concept, but there have also been some well-publicized failures. The reason service models sometimes fail

TABLE 5-1

The business benefits of function over form

Biosphere rule	Business benefit
Function over form	Generate ongoing revenue stream
	Greater customer knowledge
	Increase control over asset base
	Convergence into expanded offerings

is not because there is any inherent problem with the approach, but rather because many companies misread the role functional models play. Service models have been promoted as an end in themselves, often for purely environmental reasons. But for a company that implements the biosphere rules, it is better to see service approaches as a tool in the service of the company's sustainable platform.

As a company expands its product platform, it needs to manage the whole product system, extending beyond the factory gates into the premises of its customers. Companies no longer "sell it and forget it," but instead have an intrinsic interest in maintaining control or, in many cases, ownership of the products installed in their customers' homes and offices. In this sense, they are pursuing a functional strategy, but the primary motivation is to meet the demands of the value cycle.

Nature's Way, Business's Way

Throughout the geological record, there is wide evidence of nature's constant evolutionary experimentation with life forms. Over billions of years, nature has tried innumerable experiments to take advantage of every ecological opportunity for life to take hold. But despite the diversity of forms evident throughout geological history, there are clear patterns and similarities, especially in the roles and ecological functions organisms fulfill. In any ecosystem, there are producers and predators and there are pollinators and parasites. Each function plays an important part in the overall running of the ecosystem. A trip around the world, or at least around a zoo, shows the different ways in which those roles are filled. In North America, wolves fill the predator role taken by lions in Africa. In Australia, crepuscular, grazing marsupials like kangaroos take ecosystem slots similar to those of crepuscular grazing deer in North America. The creatures are different species, but they end up serving similar ecosystem functions.

The functions that species and their communities fulfill are incredibly important not just in sustaining their ecosystems, but also in sustaining the human economy as well. Stanford University scientist Gretchen Daily has been studying these "ecosystem services" for well over a decade. Her work documents how functions performed by species in an ecosystem collectively provide vital services such as clean water, breathable air, and a stable climate.[2] In 1997, economist Robert Costanza and colleagues, in an article in the scientific journal *Nature*, attempted to put a price on the global value of these services. Including services such as crop pollination, water purification, and so on, the annual value comes to $33 trillion each year.[3] However, as Costanza has long said, this is an underestimate of the true value.[4] The functions that species in an ecosystem fulfill are actually priceless; if the ecosystems stopped providing these services, we would all be in deep trouble. It is useful, however, to think about what nature produces at no real cost to us.

The common honeybee illustrates the economic value of the services that nature supplies. Diligent bees, in their quest for nectar in the production of honey, provide farmers an incredibly valuable service by pollinating their crops. A 2006 article in the journal *Bioscience* calculates that "insect services" in the United States alone are worth $60 billion a year.[5] But the true value of a bee's function in nature only becomes poignantly evident when the bees disappear. This is what happened in Maoxian County in Sichuan, China, where bees had done the job of pollinating the region's famous apple trees since cultivation began over seven decades ago. But starting in the 1980s, the bees began to decline and, in some cases, disappeared completely.

This spontaneous loss of honeybees has occurred over the past century in various regions, although the rate of frequency has increased since the early 1970s. In 2006, commercial bee-keepers in North America reported dramatic losses in their hives; some keepers reported losses of more than 50 percent of their hives in a single season, when historical loss rates have been less than 5 percent. The phenomenon is called colony collapse disorder (CCD), since entire colonies disappear. Scientists are unsure of its cause, but it appears to be the result of the bees being attacked by multiple pests (and pesticides) at once. But some research suggests that the problem is inbreeding—a reminder of the importance of knowledge economies. The bee colonies most affected are those that have been most inbred for efficiency as commercial pollinators. This inbreeding has limited their genetic diversity, or in other words, in the name of efficiency the bees' DNA-codified knowledge of how to survive attacks from multiple different pests simultaneously has been sacrificed.[6]

In Maoxian County, the loss of honeybees means that the only way to perpetuate the apple crop is to pollinate the trees by hand. The painstaking, labor-intensive process is repeated in the spring every year throughout the sixty-kilometer-long valley.[7] Today, however, the apple crop faces a new threat. Young people have begun to leave the villages to seek their fortunes in China's booming cities, leaving no one to pollinate the trees. Village elders fear that when they pass away, their famous apples will pass away as well.

The move to manual pollination is not limited to apples in China. In some parts of India, women have to pollinate vanilla plants by hand.[8] The lack of insect pollination services is affecting the premium ice cream maker Häagen Dazs, which calculates that 40 percent of its flavors, including vanilla, strawberry, cherry, and almond, are threatened by the disappearance of bees. Fearing a loss of its most popular flavors, Häagen Dazs is investing in research and conservation programs to highlight the causes of CCD and protect the pollinating insects so that they continue to fulfill their vital ecosystem function.[9]

The fate of honeybees illustrates how each life form is not only an individual adapted to a specific time, climatic condition, and historic circumstance, but also a member of a community providing a needed service that supports the overall health of the biosphere. At the higher ecosystem level, it is not the form the solution takes that matters, but the function. On evolutionary time scales, the biosphere does not care whether the honeybees survive. Nor for that matter does it care about ancient apple groves. But the function of pollination needs to persist through time, just not perhaps in the form of pollinating bees. This, however, is little consolation to companies like Häagen Dazs, which can't wait for the biosphere to fill the role of lost honeybees on an evolutionary time scale.

With services accounting for more than 50 percent of gross domestic product in some industrialized countries, and over 67 percent in the United States, according to the U.S. Department of Commerce, business clearly understands service models.[10]

Since the Industrial Revolution, however, economists have made a clear division between manufacturing and service industries. And service industries, in some cases, have been treated as manufacturing's ugly stepsister, of secondary importance in the quest for economic growth. In the 1980s in the United States, for example, the difference was cast in a derogatory way as "making cars" versus "flipping hamburgers."

This has changed dramatically with the technological advances at the end of the twentieth century. Modern production techniques like mass customization and flexible manufacturing have blurred some of the divisions between the service and manufacturing sectors. When Dell custom-builds a computer to meet a customer's individual needs, it adds design services to its manufacturing work. When GM financed its own car sales through its GMAC arm, it was conflating financial services with automobile manufacturing. This phenomenon is especially rampant in the information technology and communications sectors where, in a process termed "convergence," the difference between the products and the services they provide fuse and can be offered by nearly any company. An example is the search service Google, which, through offering computing software applications over the Web, threatens the business of industry gargantuan Microsoft by supplanting its software products. As companies create viable value cycles and leverage them into sustainable product platforms, they will find themselves entering into this nebulous world where products and services mingle and merge.

Rule 5: From Form to Function

Just as the biosphere's overall function is indifferent to the form community members take and depends instead on evolving solutions to biosphere-critical functions, building a sustainable product platform will shift the focus away from the form of products to the function that they are supposed to fulfill for their customers. This necessity comes as a natural consequence of successfully implementing the biosphere rules 1 through 4. Once companies have developed a sustainable product platform based on an economically viable value cycle, the traditional business model emphasis on producing and selling products will no longer serve the full needs of the business. When you are selling a product that you want to recover in the future in order to provide the needed raw materials for the next production cycle, what exactly is happening in the sales transaction? Adopting a business model that takes the recovery phase into account will encourage a shift in thinking away from traditional concern with the physical *form* through which a company delivers value and toward a more comprehensive understanding of the *functional* value it creates. In a value cycle world, it is the function that must create value for the customer, not ownership of the form.

Thus, companies that implement the biosphere rules find that their traditional roles change or become more fluid. Original manufacturers are providing a specific configuration of material assets for a temporary period of time; at the end those materials will be passed back through a value cycle and reappear as something different. In this setting, the materials in a product temporarily fulfill a function in the economy, until that function is no longer valued, and then are available to be reconfigured to fulfill new functions.

The Road to Function over Form

Implementing the biosphere rules drives companies to what researcher Walter Stahel calls the "functional economy," which he defined in 1986 as an economy that optimizes the use, or function, of goods and services and thus the management of existing wealth.[11] Around the same time, the German-based Environmental Protection Encouragement Agency (EPEA) proposed the idea of products of service. But it is straight-talking Rocky Mountain Institute founder Amory Lovins who succinctly sums up service models as "people want hot showers and cold beer" and don't really care how they get it.[12] The goal of a functional approach is to maximize the usable value of products for as long as possible, while minimizing virgin resource consumption. To do so, economic agents move from a focus on mass producing disposable consumption goods and turn instead to providing durable products that produce problem-solving results.

Environmentalists have favored functional models because of their ability to align incentives toward more efficient and less environmentally damaging outcomes. The classic example is a seller of car paints. In a transactional model, the company wants to sell as many cans of paint as possible to maximize revenues. But if the seller is instead providing the function of painted cars and is thus paid per vehicle and not per gallon of paint sold, the incentives change. Now profit maximization depends on the paint seller minimizing the costs of the paint used, which should unleash managerial creativity to find innovative ways of providing a beautiful car finish with a minimum of paint usage and waste. In many cases, a shift to a functional approach can achieve this serendipitous alignment of incentives.

Researchers at the economic and environmental think tank Tellus Institute have termed this transition from product-oriented to service-oriented business models *servicization*.[13] They propose a variety of strategies for organizing a service approach, often emphasizing the creation of agreements that in many ways resemble a traditional lease. For the provider of services, there are theoretical benefits of moving to a functional model. The long-term, ongoing nature of arrangements such as leases can allow a provider to get closer to the customer and gives it the opportunity to provide ongoing value over the life of the product, a dynamic that can encourage an extended and profitable relationship. It furthermore creates the possibility of identifying additional value-adding services that can accompany the product.

A few of the product manufacturers discussed in previous chapters have found it expedient to move to a functional model. Xerox, for example, derives over three-quarters of its revenues from leasing its equipment and associated services.[14] When the company began discussing the strategy publicly, it described it this way: "Everything that Xerox delivers to its customers is designed to be returned—whether it is a machine, cartridge, a spare or packaging. All of these items, once returned, are processed for reuse and recycling. The only thing we want to leave our customer is—*the document*."[15] The strategy has driven Xerox to focus on maximizing the profitability of customer relationships by continually offering value-added services, not maximizing the number of products pushed out the door. The pallet company iGPS is similarly managing a product base that is loaned out to fulfill a customer's shipping need, but is then recovered for the next job, leaving their customers with only their delivered goods.

The Function-Product Convergence

In some industries, there is a process of convergence, with product-oriented sectors moving to a functional model, and vice versa. Castrol, part of the BP Group of companies, is a maker of performance lubricants and motor oil. But in the late 1990s, Castrol realized it had far more to offer customers than just lubricant in a drum: it had valuable, specialized knowledge and expertise about lubricant performance and applications that customers could never develop in-house. So instead of just selling its product by the barrel, the company created Castrol Industrial, a services division dedicated to developing long-term partnerships with lubricant users. Castrol Industrial provided customers with trained sales engineers who would analyze customers' equipment, processes, and production materials and then make specialized recommendations about the appropriate Castrol products and applications. In addition, Castrol Industrial created a new service offering called Castrol Complete that provides a full range of lubricant-related functions: chemical handling training, environmental reporting, regulatory compliance, and end-of-life recovery and regeneration or recycling of Castrol products. With the service emphasis, Castrol's key value proposition to its customers shifted from selling a product toward helping to reduce customers' net operating costs.

In addition to the closer customer relationships Castrol was able to foster, the company also derived other business gains from its functional model. Profits, for example, were generated from two sources. The first came from service fees, which Castrol collected as part of its specialized consulting and process improvement analysis. But Castrol also developed an innovative contractual relationship that shares the benefits of cost reductions attained from using Castrol services. This not only provides a whole new revenue stream for Castrol based on reducing the use of its products (now there's a business model!), but it also reassures the customer that Castrol's services are aimed at mutual benefit, not just selling the customer more stuff. In one case, the client company was able to reduce the amount of product it was using by 50 percent and was further able to reduce waste by 90 percent. Finally, in some instances, Castrol is able to establish product reprocessing and regeneration capabilities at the customer's site, effectively creating a deep-loop value cycle on the premises—improving both Castrol's and the customer's bottom line. Castrol is not alone in this movement toward a functional model. A 2004 survey estimates that "chemical management services" is a $1.2 billion business, operating in eleven different industrial sectors from autos to steel.[16] Interestingly, three quarters of the companies operating in the segment were originally chemical product manufactures. One quarter of the players, however, are pure service players, producing no product of their own, just selling their sophisticated expertise in product use.

This shows that convergence can go both ways. In some service industries, for example, companies are migrating—or in some cases returning—to providing equipment and appliances that work with their service. Electric, gas, and water utilities are an example. The Spanish power utility Iberdrola, for example, has become not only a provider of electricity and gas but a vendor of select high-efficiency appliances and a designer of building energy systems.[17] The company has established retail outlets and showrooms in major Spanish cities to sell energy-efficient appliances and to provide home and office energy system consulting. Customers can speak with an Iberdrola expert who will assess their current energy situation and recommend a combination of heating, air conditioning, and cooking products that ensure maximum functional benefit for their energy expenditures. Iberdrola also offers financing and insurance for its customers' purchases. And they are not alone. Iberdrola's competitor Endesa has also opened their own competing showrooms across the Iberian Penninsula, launching their own integrated offerings.

On the other side of the world in Toyama Prefecture, Japan, Nihonkai Gas Co., Ltd. provides a similar example. The company had a history of selling customers heaters for their homes, but in 2001, managers reasoned that what customers really wanted in the winter was the warmth the heaters provided, not the device itself. So instead of selling the heaters, the company began renting them seasonally for ¥3,000, about $25. Customers embraced the service, and the company found that demand for rented heaters outstripped its initial targets. One of the biggest advantages for customers living in cramped Tokyo apartments is that Nihonkai Gas picks up the heater when spring arrives and takes it back to its warehouse. While the heaters are in the warehouse, Nihonkai inspects them thoroughly and performs maintenance, which extends their working life and ensures that they operate at peak efficiency.[18]

Examples like these demonstrate that function-based models can be approached from either the product or the service side. They also suggest potentially interesting opportunities for service companies and product providers to collaborate. But while businesses have pursued functional or service models for their own sake, for companies implementing the biosphere rules, a more nuanced understanding of the role of functional models in creating a sustainable product platform is required, as the following cautionary tale indicates.

A Rush to Function

Interface, the world's largest manufacturer of commercial carpet tile, is a well-known early mover in functional business models. Interface CEO Ray Anderson's public statements about sustainability in the 1990s motivated many companies, including Interface competitor Shaw Industries, to make sustainability a core business challenge. Corporate lore holds that Anderson was influenced by Paul Hawken's book, *The Ecology of Commerce*, which among other cutting-edge concepts promoted the idea of "licensing products of service."[19] Anderson wondered if the approach could be applied to carpet tile, allowing Interface to offer "floor covering services" instead of selling flooring products.

Turning carpet from a product into a service presented tantalizing opportunities, but more than a few challenges. Interface's strategy was to offer a flooring service in which it guaranteed that it would maintain the carpet in excellent condition. The company would clean and inspect the carpet periodically and replace any worn-out tiles with new ones. Recognizing that carpet wear was subject to the eighty/twenty rule, that is, 80 percent of the carpet wear occurred on the 20 percent of carpet exposed in high-traffic areas, by replacing only the worn-out tiles, Interface could reduce waste and save money. Furthermore, Interface hoped offering a service would foster closer, longer-term customer relationships and a more predictable revenue stream.

Interface settled on a leasing strategy, figuring that this would be the easiest transition for their customers, since many already leased their office equipment. In 1995, the company inaugurated the Evergreen Lease, to substantial positive press and public accolades. The logic of the approach, however, ran into trouble with customers and especially customers' accountants. In effect, carpet did not fit the Financial Accounting Standards Board (FASB) requirements for an operating lease. The FASB deemed that an operating lease should extend for less than 75 percent of the estimated economic life of the product.

Furthermore, the total value of the lease payments needed to be less than the fair-market cost of buying the product, and the product had to be worth at least 15 percent of its original value when the lease ended.[20]

Valuing end-of-life carpet turned out to be a real challenge. As Interface vice president Eric Nelson put it, unlike valuing used cars, "there's no Kelly Blue Book price for used carpet."[21] With over 95 percent of end-of-life carpet ending up in landfills, it was hard to make the argument that the residual value of carpet was more than zero (in fact, technically it might be considered a liability, since you had to pay someone to haul it away), let alone 15 percent of the original purchase price. What Interface thought was a clever innovation to smooth the transition to sustainability for itself and its customers foundered, as company after company balked at carpet leasing.

The Function of Functional Models

The inability to sell customers on the idea of leasing carpet has been used as an argument against functional models as a business strategy, but that is an overreach. The truth is that Interface didn't get it wrong; it just jumped the gun, something that company executives freely admit. By heeding the advice to plunge into a service model when it did, Interface put the cart before the horse. In 1995, Interface did not have the economic technologies and processes to allow it to effectively value-cycle its carpet tiles, which meant waste carpet had no salvage value. But since the days of the Evergreen Lease, a lot has changed. Today, Interface has arguably one of the most comprehensive sustainable product platforms around.

From the beginning of its sustainability strategy, Interface had value cycling in mind. According to John Bradford, vice president of operations and R&D, "If you look at the tenets of sustainability, it's about the materials that we use, the process that we use to get those, and the energy we expend in the process. Ray Anderson asked 'What it would take to bend the linear take-make-waste system around into a cyclical system that looked something like what happened in nature?'"[22] Doing so required about a decade's worth of innovation. The result is five patented technologies that make up the company's sustainable product platform.

As illustrated in figure 5-1, the first are a pair of process technologies: Convert, which value-cycles the soft nylon face fiber

FIGURE 5-1

The interface value cycle

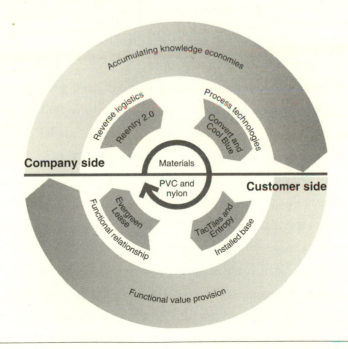

walking surface, and Cool Blue, which value-cycles the heavy vinyl (PVC) backing. In 2005, Interface began running the Cool Blue vinyl process partially with renewable landfill biogas, moving the company to the frontier of power autonomy. However, by choosing to value-cycle PVC, Interface is fighting a trend away from PVC by some competitors because PVC can produce toxic by-products. But the industry has been producing vinyl carpet tiles since 1973; there are literally tens of billions of pounds of the material in the marketplace. According to Bradford, "Seventy-five percent of the carpet coming off the floor today is PVC, and many companies are running away from it. In our minds, we have a responsibility to figure out what to do with all that material out there."[23] The company argues that the hazards of PVC arise when it is originally manufactured or improperly disposed of. By keeping it in a closed-loop value cycle, it eliminates the most hazardous stages of the life cycle. Beyond the responsibility argument, there is also a business attraction: if competitors abandon the material, Interface is unlikely to face competition for recovered vinyl tiles.

In addition to the materials and associated process technologies, Interface has three other innovations that improve value cycle economics. Along with a reinvigorated Evergreen Lease are two innovations that facilitate the service-provision phase of the value cycle and assist in delivering functional value. TacTiles is a carpet-installation technology that eliminates gluing and eases installation and removal. This is a facilitating innovation that enables rapid flow from one part of the value cycle to the next. Then there is Entropy, a new design approach for the pattern and coloring of floor tiles, which allows easy substitution between different dye lots. Entropy is a biomimicry innovation inspired by the nature's carpeting produced by foliage alighting on the forest floor during a New England fall. Finally, Interface's most recent innovation is ReEntry 2.0, a process that cleanly separates the backing from the face fiber. Collectively this suite of innovations has created an economical sustainable product platform at Interface that did not exist when the company launched its original Evergreen Lease in 1995. Today, Interface can value-cycle both the backing and the face fiber of its carpet in cost-effective ways.

These innovations change the equation for Interface. First, the company can now demonstrate that the end-of-life carpet is worth more than 15 percent of the purchase price, based on its ability to use the waste carpet as an input. This satisfies the FASB and makes it easier to create a viable leasing strategy; Interface is indeed considering a renewed leasing effort. But whether or not the company's carpet tiles meet expectations for a leasing arrangement, the fundamental issue is that Interface will want its old tiles back to serve as raw materials for the next production run, no matter what. And for companies like Interface that implement the biosphere rules, this is a key driver of a functional model.

"Custopliers" and "Supplustomers"

It should be obvious at this point that the functional or service model is an inevitable outcome of creating a sustainable product platform. While money may make the world go 'round, in order for a value cycle to function properly, materials have to come back to the producer in good condition and in a time frame that suits production needs. This in turn creates a demand for greater control over all stages of the value cycle. One stage, however, stands out over the others—the customer use stage. In effect, as seen in figure 5-1, customers become an integral part of Interface's value cycle: as both recipients of the product benefits and also suppliers of the manufacturer's input materials. They become *custopliers* and *supplustomers*. They are members of the company's production network, embedded in its value cycle. As Kevin Kelley, founding editor of *Wired* magazine, observed about the network economy, "Outsiders act as employees, employees act as outsiders. New relationships blur the roles of employees and customers to the point of unity. They reveal the customer and the company as one."[24] Managing this new relationship becomes a key aspect of value chain design.

How value cycling changes the game can be seen by comparing a home builder and an hotelier. A home builder sells his customer twenty-five hundred square feet of architecturally aesthetic wood, glass, and tile that in transfer becomes the customer's full responsibility. The focus of the developer's business is on the one-time transaction and the hand-off of product ownership and responsibility. A hotel stay, in contrast, involves the temporary provision of space and lodging service. A customer doesn't buy the room. Instead he purchases the provisional benefit of protection from rain and cold, a place to drop his travel bags, and a warm bed. The hotel owner fully expects to recover the room and resell it (temporarily) to the next visitor who needs it. But the hotelier does not see this as a one-time transaction either. She also wants the first customer to have positive emotional impressions and experiences so she can resell a room to him the next time he is in town. Good hotel managers know that their establishments provide psychic and emotional benefits that go beyond simply four walls and a roof. By providing additional value in the form of attentive staff, a hip lobby, a swanky bar, and a quality dinner, they hope to provide an intangible emotional payoff that enchants customers and keeps them coming back.

Product manufacturers that fully implement the biosphere rules will become more like hoteliers than home builders. Like the hotel room, they expect and need to get their products back. But they also hope to resell the materials embedded in their products to the same customer when he or she has a functional need for the company's goods in the future. The fundamental transaction between business and customer is no longer an exchange of ownership. It is an exchange of service facilitated through the use of the seller's material assets embodied in its products.

Of course, while service models can theoretically apply to anything, not all products are best served by a service model that establishes a leasing-type arrangement. The goal is to maintain control and access to the materials, something that can be done in many ways. Disposables and consumables like foodstuffs, diapers, toothbrushes, and even packaging have limited servicization possibilities. Selling people "tooth-brushing service," while possible, is unlikely to generate overwhelming customer response. For products in these categories, a better strategy is found less in creating a service model and more in focusing on creating a highly efficient deep-loop value cycle for these products and finding other ways to ensure return of the end-of-use products.

Choosing a Functional Relationship

From the operational side, there are a number of ways that companies can structure functional relationships with clients. Most companies already have warranties, guarantees, and limited service agreements associated with their products. And most product-based companies have customer service and after-sales service experience. Thus, the simplest starting point for most companies is to look at their existing warranties and service agreements for opportunities. Often they can be revised or extended to serve value cycle needs and provide avenues for ensuring the return of products and materials.

An interesting example is California-based Pelican Industries' lifetime guarantee. Pelican manufactures high-performance protective cases for precision equipment, from cameras to sporting rifles. Each sale of a Pelican case comes with a lifetime guarantee in which the company promises to repair or replace a damaged case. Companies often use lifetime guarantees to assure customers of the durability and quality of products. In some cases, the guarantee is more a marketing tool than a real effort to stand behind a product; the terms and conditions associated with the warranty make it virtually impossible to return the product. Pelican, however, has implemented a lifetime guarantee without conditions in order to serve the needs of a value cycle. Pelican has a deep-loop process that can take back and recycle the materials in its damaged or end-of-life cases and turn them into new Pelican products.

While warranties may be a useful starting point for some companies, most are still built around the traditional transfer-of-ownership model. However, companies with well-developed product platforms and value cycles may prefer not to transfer ownership of products to their customers. In these cases, companies may turn to contractual provisions that require the customer to return the product to the company at the end of use, as we saw in the printer cartridge business. Alternatively, companies can create incentives for the return of their products by offering discounts on new purchases or other return rewards. In 2005, for example, Apple began offering customers the opportunity to return an old iPod and get a 10 percent discount on the purchase of a new iPod the same day.[25]

Leasing can also be a way to achieve these goals. When most people think of leasing in a business context, however, they are thinking of capital leases, which are widely used because they provide tax advantages. Accountants basically treat capital leases, which serve as financing vehicles, as loans. At the end of a capital lease, ownership of the product usually passes automatically to the lessee. This is exactly the opposite of what companies that have implemented the biosphere rules want to happen.

For companies with a value cycle in place, a better alternative is an operating lease, which is also known as a true lease. In an operating lease, ownership generally stays with the lessor, which recovers the product at the end of the contract. In this sense, the operating lease is a vehicle for creating a contractual and lasting relationship with customers. It provides opportunities to expand services and product provision over the life of the relationship, while simultaneously helping a company meet the demands of its value cycle. Operating leases are well suited to delivering functional value while maintaining asset ownership, as the Interface example illustrates, but they are not without challenges.

In addition to the barriers imposed by accounting standards, leasing faces another challenge: a significant stigma in many people's minds. For some, leasing is associated with accounting tricks to reduce tax liabilities through the use of excessively high financing rates. Others view it as a second-best option to actually owning a product. Companies pursuing leasing strategies may have to confront and counter these perceptions in the marketplace.

However, a talented marketing department can make the benefits of leasing for customers a convincing business proposition. Advantages such as the option of paying over time instead of making a large one-time investment—effectively gaining nearly 100 percent financing of the product—and the flexibility in structuring the finances to account for cash flow and changing financial conditions can be important to many customers. Companies also can highlight service features: customers don't have to deal with the hassle of in-house maintenance, insurance, or the costly upgrading that comes with ownership. In addition, customers have the comfort of not feeling locked into a purchase decision, especially in rapidly evolving technologies, and the possibility of ongoing value-added services that enhance the customer experience over the long haul.

The Management Challenges of Functional Approaches

Internally, the shift from a product or transactional model to a functional business model involves a cultural change that will affect everyone, from product designers to finance, marketing, sales, and senior management. The root of the challenge lies in the fact that in a functional sales model, the company no longer generates profits from sales, but from service fees. Financial analysts like service models, because a service contract usually means an ongoing source of income, as opposed to a one-and-done transaction. This is particularly true in sectors where the costs of customer acquisition and retention are trending up. Despite the favorable impression service financing gives to outside observers, however, it stands in opposition to the standard product sales model in most companies, which rewards sales personnel based on how many units or packages they sell. Sales oriented in this manner are discrete and tangible, and thus easy to measure, track, and reward.

In shifting from "sell it and forget it" approaches, companies will be helped by developing and adopting managerial and accounting tools better suited to the task. One tool some have adopted to emphasize long-term customer satisfaction over short-term sales is the customer lifetime value (CLV) concept, which measures value as the future sum of cash flows coming from a customer relationship. Instead of increasing revenue through new one-time sales, the approach focuses on revenue streams over time. While not foolproof, CLV is an example of management tools and thinking that companies implementing the biosphere rules can explore.

Beyond the tools, most companies will need to shift the transaction-oriented mind-set of salespeople. The skills needed to sell a product once are different from those needed to maintain an ongoing service relationship. It is somewhat akin to the difference in the service a bank teller provides and that provided by the bank's financial adviser. One is completing a transaction, while the other is focused on developing a relationship, with the accompanying psycho-social dynamics. Adjusting the reward and compensation structures to account for service interactions, as well as providing the proper training, will help talented, flexible salespeople make the leap, but inevitable attrition must be expected.

Despite the challenges to the company culture, shifting organizational mentality is in some ways the easy part. Potential difficulties also lie in influencing people outside the company—that is, customers—and helping them see the value they will get from the change. Because customers are deeply steeped in value chain consumption, they are not used to thinking of things like washing their clothes at home in terms of the total cost incurred in the process. A customer can easily grasp the high upfront cost of purchasing a washer and dryer, but it is far more difficult to calculate and understand the daily and periodic costs accrued from the electricity and water—utilities that are billed in total, not by appliance—as well as unit costs of detergent, maintenance, and repair charges on their home equipment, or the cost of their own lost productivity. Given all these hidden costs, laundry service fees may seem astronomical to a client who has no experience with them, when in reality, they may be less than the true total cost of ownership of a washing machine and dryer. Interface encountered this service "sticker shock" when it presented Evergreen Lease proposals to commercial clients. Most customers had no idea of the true cost to the company of purchasing, maintaining, and upgrading flooring, mostly because the costs were divided into different accounts like capital, maintenance, and overhead.

This challenge can be ameliorated through client education. In some industries, useful information technology tools are becoming viable to help with education, such as smart household and office appliance metering systems and networking that allow customers to see the true cost of ownership, often in real time. Cost transparency and immediate feedback can be a powerful way to influence customer behavior and understanding. Managerial tools like activity-based accounting and full-cost accounting that disaggregate and assign expenditures to their source and thus more accurately account for the total costs of an activity will also help customers make more informed decisions. Industry associations can also help create better awareness in the market place. For example, the Chemical Strategies Partnership (CSP), a nonprofit in San Francisco dedicated to the adoption of service models for chemical use, has built customer information tools like a computer-based chemical management cost-assessment program that lays bare the full costs of chemical management and how much can be saved by moving to a functional provision model.

There are also other, more subtle psychological dynamics at play on the customer side. Some products like sports cars transfer identity, status, and other benefits that are difficult to calculate into a service arrangement. Marketers thus have an important role in ensuring that a company's products serve not only functional needs but also the psychological and emotional needs of customers. This includes addressing customer concerns over ownership and property rights issues that emerge when companies transition from selling products to providing services. None of these potential impediments are permanent, of course. Customer attitudes and expectations evolve over time. Fostering this kind of attitudinal change has to be embedded in the new marketing proposition that a company moving to function from form makes to its customers.

And as I have seen repeatedly, the shift also has consequences for product design teams. Until now, the focus on design teams has been to ensure their work facilitated the efficient and economic functioning of the sustainable product platform. But designers can also play a valuable role in both enhancing the customer experience through superior product design and enhancing the value cycle benefits, as the next section shows.

Human Factors Design

This chapter has focused mostly on how to rethink products in terms of the functions they provide to customers, but the functional approach can go farther, in some cases to a point at which the actual product might be unnecessary. The work of design studio IDEO, located in Silicon Valley, California, suggests some interesting alternatives. IDEO has become a go-to source for design-driven firms like Apple and Procter & Gamble when they are seeking product and service innovations. Companies come to IDEO for its unique innovation methodology, which emphasizes human factors in design.

Instead of beginning with the design of a physical product, the company begins by examining the behavior the product will affect. How people actually interact with and utilize products and the social milieu in which they are used are considered crucial design information. To get this information, IDEO employs the techniques of anthropologists, archeologists, and behavioral scientists by observing, excavating, and documenting users' actions in the field. IDEO professionals can spend up to 20 percent or more of project time just watching what their target customers do on a day-to-day basis. This differs from more traditional research techniques such as surveys and focus groups, which can be misleading because people often behave differently in context than they say they do. Intention and behavior often diverge, especially when money is on the line. IDEO's innovation methodology thus relies heavily on how people really act. By observing them in real interactions, IDEO can develop insights that neither the potential innovation users nor the IDEO client could have predicted.

The global banking giant Bank of America experienced this firsthand. It came to IDEO with a problem: customers weren't using their debit cards enough. They were instead relying on checks and credit cards, which carried higher processing costs for the bank than debit transactions. To decrease these costs, Bank of America wanted to create incentives for its customers to use debit cards over other forms of payment. The bank's initial idea was to give out a money clip with a slot in which to embed the debit card so that the card would be first thing the customer saw when paying. A clever idea, but was designing, manufacturing, and distributing tens of thousands of money clips really the best way to address the problem?

IDEO stepped in with an ethnographic research study. It invited Bank of America representatives to join in a field research effort aimed at better understanding customers' behavior. The target market turned out to be "soccer mom" types—boomer-generation mothers with children. IDEO employees, along with representatives from Bank of America's innovation team, observed their target customers at multiple sites around the country. As they watched them engage in their daily family and financial routines, they noticed some interesting behavior. Many of the women were struggling with their finances and finding it hard to save money for things like college or retirement. Also, when balancing checkbooks and transactions, many customers would round up to the nearest whole number. Apparently this was faster and more convenient and provided a buffer to prevent overdrawn accounts.

Armed with observations, IDEO returned to Bank of America, not with a product but a new service called "Keep the Change." The service, provided to holders of a Bank of America debit card, would automatically round up purchases made with the card. The difference would be transferred directly from the customer's checking account into a savings account, automating the process of saving. This would simultaneously provide a needed financial buffer while helping families save for the future.

After extensive prototyping, testing, and refinement, Keep the Change made its debut in October 2005. Within a year, the service had 2.5 million subscribers. Of these, 1.7 million were new accounts for Bank of America. Keep the Change was widely recognized in the press and among banking professionals, and was awarded the Outstanding Corporate Innovator Award by the Product Development and Management Association in 2006.

The IDEO example indicates how focusing on behavior and functional needs can lead to alternative ways of solving a customer's problem. IDEO's Steve Bishop likes to refer to Harvard Business School marketing professor Theodore Levitt's maxim, "People who buy drills don't need drills; they need holes."[26] Bank of America and IDEO found a way to solve a customer's problem by adding new functionality to an existing product, not provide a new plastic widget.

The focus on selling products, and not the function they fill, has been dominant for the past sixty years and is a formidable obstacle to managers seeking to implement the fifth biosphere rule. It's the reason that this rule is the last and, for most managers, the hardest to achieve. However, it is a crucial rule to understand and pursue, because function over form is not just a path to increasing profits. Function over form also reveals the harsher side of nature, a side that nature shares with competitive markets.

Function over form means that right now you have competitors that you've never even thought of—competitors that are performing a similar function in other industries or context with a completely different solution. Product-centric thinking creates barriers between industries that function over form will tear down. I noted at the beginning of the chapter that nature does not care which species performs the necessary functions, only that those functions get fulfilled. You'll quickly discover that if you're slow off the mark in the conversion to function over form, your customers and the market will prove similarly merciless when a brand new competitor comes along and meets functional needs and, like the IDEO example, makes your product disappear.

As with the other biosphere rules we've examined, there will be plenty of temptations and justifications for letting others move first, for waiting to see what technology and regulatory developments are on the horizon before committing to action. "Wait and see" may seem like a safe and prudent approach. It's not. In the biosphere, those who wait and see will watch more efficient users of resources and energy and more effective deliverers of services fill their niche. If ever there was an appropriate time to invoke dinosaurs as a business analogy, this is it. The world is changing and the mammals are coming. It's time to make the choice to evolve.

Conclusion

Building the Ecosystem

Nature is amazingly productive. It has evolved millions of species from a handful of basic elements. It builds virtuous value cycles in which those millions of species fill the roles of producers, consumers, and decomposers, and product and waste alike are integrated and recycled. It leverages those cycles through reproduction and speciation, and shares survival know-how through DNA. It taps into inherently renewable energy sources and builds internal systems for autonomous access and use of that energy. And no matter what, it ensures that all essential functions are fulfilled so its systems and cycles are always serviced. This is what makes the biosphere's innovation and productivity dwarf our own.

Natural systems, however, are also destructive. While Joseph Schumpeter is credited with coining the term "creative destruction," nature is the inventor of the concept. Nature ensures that its system of production, consumption, and decomposition survives and thrives, but it is neutral about the continuation of any individual player or species in the mix. In a sense, nature is the world's most efficient market. When a particular participant in the natural world is failing to use available resources efficiently, nature will, without sentiment, evolve a replacement that will.

The way in which species become extinct is not always fair. After all, nature is cooperative in its productivity. In hostile desert environments, the survival of many flora and fauna in an oasis depends on the shade provided by palms that grow in the cracks where water previously managed to trickle and reside. If the palms die, everything might follow, even those species that are doing the best to use available resources to greatest effect.

The same is true for business. Companies that do not respond to the changing market dynamics and the changing availability of inputs will be starved into extinction. Perhaps they will be replaced by companies that do know how to operate better within the new constraints. Even businesses that are doing all the right things might end up threatened because they operate in an ecosystem that is still struggling with green growth.

No company or product is an island. Even the most vertically integrated business depends on a huge number of relationships with customers, communities, regulators, and suppliers of energy and other needs. The five biosphere rules show how companies can structure value cycle relationships that foster increasing returns for their product platform. But all products and business must be seen as part of larger systems that go beyond a single value cycle. As a consequence, no company can be sustainable by itself. Most of the case studies of successful green growth we've looked at include either suppliers or customers or both. Ultimately, the expansion of green growth beyond a product line or platform will require involvement of an entire business ecosystem.

Fostering Succession—Changing the Ecosystem

For most managers seeking to apply the rules of the biosphere, ensuring that they are part of a mutually beneficial ecosystem inside and outside their organization will be critical to success. As you pursue green growth, you'll need to watch those around you and seek ways to influence and integrate your efforts with peers, suppliers, customers, and even competitors.

For some, this will happen naturally. After all, new innovations that change the landscape of business occur all the time. Historically, it's new upstart companies bringing disruptive technologies to market. The producers of vacuum tube technology did not commercialize transistor technology. AT&T didn't originally champion the cellular phone. General Motors, once the largest car company in the world and the first to put a modern electric car on the market, missed out on hybrids. In all these cases, the previous market leaders didn't believe the opportunities were there until new entrants came along and capitalized on them. The tunnel vision of leading players happens in part because existing investments in traditional products and technologies, and commitments to current business practice, often create tacit or overt disincentives for aggressively promoting change that will disrupt existing businesses. One of the reasons that compact fluorescent lightbulbs, for example, have achieved only 6 percent penetration in the United States, despite the fact that they use 75 percent less energy and last ten times longer, is because aggressive promotion would cannibalize the existing incandescent bulb business.

And yet change is inevitable; just look to nature. New ecosystems—like a pine forest or an alpine meadow—develop through a gradual process known as succession, where colonizing species alter the local environment and make it hospitable to a larger, more diverse community of organisms. In a mature, tropical rain forest, for example, the soils usually are thin and low in nutrients. This is because the vast majority of the system's resources are stored in the canopy of trees. A change in conditions, from a forest fire, for example, or a change in weather patterns, releases the resources and makes them available to new organisms. The community then goes through a reorganization process that will create a new and different ecosystem.

This process of release and restructuring—of creative destruction—is what keeps the biosphere productive and allows it to fill even the most extreme environments. Businesses pursuing green growth are undertaking innovations that can foster similar creative destruction in their industries. Managers don't have to wait for conditions to change, however, because business doesn't respond only to the external environment. It also can actively influence its development. Managers can deploy three approaches to building the necessary supportive ecosystems so that they end up on the right side of creative destruction: niche strategies, keystone species, and acts of God.

Niche Strategies

Finding space to make a living in an ecosystem is the job of every species, and nature is exceptionally adept at it. Through innovation, life finds unique ways to take advantage of nearly every ecosystem opportunity. A classic 1958 study of wood warblers by the naturalist R. H. MacArthur found that five different species of the bird could live in a single tree. By nesting at different levels and pursuing distinct food sources, each species could eke out a separate living.[1] Companies can utilize similar niche strategies to establish a foothold for their green products and services.

Thomas Edison pursued just such a strategy for his innovations. To demonstrate electric lighting, for example, Edison sought niches in small, self-contained locations. One of his first applications was to install incandescent lightbulbs on ocean-going ships. This allowed him to demonstrate a complete lighting system including generator, distribution wires, and bulbs. Edison then expanded his demonstration by installing the first city lighting in a place where it would be sure to attract needed attention: Wall Street. By craftily installing lighting there, he maximized exposure to investors and city officials.[2] From Edison's electrical systems emerged a vibrant ecosystem of lighting appliances, entertainment, equipment, and dozens of other products and related industries.

An example of strategically pursuing a niche strategy can also be seen in the establishment of the Danish wind turbine industry. Denmark is a clear leader in wind energy, and Danish companies like Vestas currently command about half of the world market for turbines. Wind turbines got their start when small producers experimented with turbines in the 1970s. By the 1980s, significant local know-how had developed, and lobbying by the manufacturers brought government support of the industry. Within this niche, a Danish wind industry developed that has since expanded globally.

Niche strategies also apply within companies. Shaw's EcoWorx project, Clorox's Green Works, and 3M's energy efficiency drive all started as niche products or projects. By capturing attention and demonstrating bottom-line value, managers at each of these companies were able to build senior management support and get the whole company behind their efforts.

Niche strategies make the most sense for companies and/or products that will initially appeal to environmentally conscious consumers. Niche strategies allow young companies to fly under the radar of the established brands, which often do not regard smaller niche markets as much of an opportunity or threat. This gives companies time for experimentation and learning that, with a savvy eye toward transition, can help them cross into mainstream markets.

Keystone Species

Niche strategies allow innovators to organically grow a product or market from the ground up. With an awareness of emerging opportunities, products can expand beyond their niches. Some entrepreneurs don't have patience to wait for niches to grow. These players instead find ways to inject green growth DNA into existing industries. New Leaf Paper's founder Jeff Mendelsohn is just such an entrepreneur. He broke into his field using the keystone species approach.

A keystone in architecture is the stone at the apex of an arch that locks the other pieces together. A keystone species in biology is one that, while often low in numbers, has an unduly large impact on its environment. Beavers, for example, tend to have a low population in any ecosystem where they are found, but they have a big impact on the environment when they create a dam in a river. The pond created as a consequence of the dam significantly alters the local environment and fosters several new niches for species to colonize. Mendelsohn has achieved a comparable feat in the paper industry.

His plan was straightforward. New Leaf wanted to produce sustainably manufactured paper products, but owned no production capacity of its own. So Mendelsohn decided to source sustainably produced paper from existing mills. To do so, New Leaf needed to find a supplier willing to use manufacturing processes that met New Leaf's sustainability criteria. One company that fulfilled New Leaf's standards for sustainable production was Denmark's Dalum Papir. Dalum already had substantial sustainability knowledge and production capabilities. It had created its own value cycling process that could take waste paper, de-ink it, and use it for feedstock for new paper. The plant was also located close to the supply of urban waste near Copenhagen, ensuring easy access to input. New Leaf worked with Dalum to step up the sustainability of its paper producing processes, calling for the use of clean chemistry and chlorine-free production.

The partnership with Dalum and other paper mills helped New Leaf overcome its supply challenge. But it still needed to seek out demand if it was to succeed. New Leaf worked with potential customers to create sustainable paper products that met their needs. Initially it partnered with companies like Aveda and Seeds of Change that had made environmental responsibility part of their business vision. Niche markets like these are not enough for a player looking to have a keystone impact, however, so New Leaf began partnering with companies like Hewlett-Packard and IKEA to expand its market. In 1997, it hooked up with Bank of America, which at the time was interested in improving its green purchasing practices. The bank used huge quantities of paper and thus was an interesting potential market. To realize the potential, New Leaf and Bank of America collaborated to create a paper product called New Leaf Everest. It was the first 100 percent post-consumer waste, high-quality letterhead paper.

Since the 1997 collaboration with Bank of America, New Leaf has developed a succession of innovative paper products, with each generation upping the green ante. In 2001, it developed EcoBook 100, the first 100 percent post-consumer waste, chlorine-free, book paper. In May 2003, nearly a million copies of *Harry Potter and the Order of the Phoenix* were printed on EcoBook 100. Today, New Leaf's customers include such leaders as Starbucks, Stanford University, Republic of Tea, and Office Depot. New Leaf continues to find innovative ways to foster growth of the market. To create market awareness of sustainable paper, the company provides certificates that demonstrate the "greenness" of paper choices. Certification documents how many trees, water, energy, waste, and greenhouse gases were avoided by purchasing New Leaf paper. Companies then put this information on their Web sites and marketing collateral to raise the awareness and publicize the benefits of green paper. All this, of course, intensifies consumer knowledge and interest in green paper products like New Leaf's.

New Leaf's understanding of green growth extends beyond building its own sales. The company's strategy of not owning the mills or other assets has the benefit of allowing New Leaf to lower the costs of product development and ensure that the company's green designs will not be encumbered by past commitments. The risk, however, is that because New Leaf shares its designs with paper manufacturers, it loses the ability to protect its innovations as company trade secrets. This means innovations are easily imitated. It has often been the case that New Leaf's own mill partners do the imitating and launch their own competing product. After the Harry Potter success of EcoBook 100, for example, three different companies launched competing green book-paper products. This doesn't particularly bother Mendelsohn, though. The company's mission statement says that its "goal is to inspire—through our success—a fundamental shift toward environmental responsibility in the paper indus-try."[3] Imitation is the greatest form of flattery. In this sense, New Leaf is truly behaving as a keystone species and altering the con-ditions for an entire industry.

Act of God—The Green Walmart Effect

A select group of existing players—based on their size and influence—have the potential to affect their business ecosystems much more dramatically than niche or keystone players can. With over $300 billion in sales, for instance, Walmart's decisions can have repercussions across industries, sectors, nations, and even the global economy. The scale of Walmart's reach is mas-sive. When its sales are compared to gross domestic product of countries, the company emerges as the twentieth largest eco-nomic entity on the planet, larger financially than countries like Denmark and Sweden. Thus when Walmart requests changes from an industry, the impact is less like that of a keystone species and more like an act of God.

In July 2009, Walmart caused major waves throughout the business community when it announced an initiative to create a sustainability index for all the products it sold. The goal is to cre-ate a system so that customers could judge the sustainability of a bag of snacks alongside its nutritional content. The scale will pur-portedly measure such items as water and power consumed in making the product, as well as such items as compliance with labor standards.[4] Walmart's announcement has already set off a cascade effect in many markets—to provide the information Wal-mart will demand, suppliers have to in-turn gather reams of data from their own suppliers on the components of the sustainability index. But no one should have been surprised at the wide-reaching effect of Walmart's announcement. Walmart has a history of radically changing the sustainability context.

In 2005, Walmart's senior management team committed the company to a new vision of sustainability. Walmart's CEO Lee Scott set impressive sustainability targets, including the use of 100 percent renewable energy, generating zero waste, and selling only sustainable products, achieving these goals between 2010 and 2025. While laudable goals, they are virtually unachievable without the active cooperation of Walmart's more than sixty thousand suppliers. By its own account, impact from Walmart's direct operations was a mere 10 percent of the total impact created by the company's sourcing and supply chain decisions. Walmart could not be sustainable by itself. It has to have a strategy to influence its suppliers, customers, and entire related industries to create sustainable product solutions.

To achieve its vision, Walmart has set out to change how business is done in fourteen of what it calls "value networks." These networks include industries such as textiles, electronics, jewelry, and seafood, as well as renewable energy. Also included are entire countries, like China. Within these networks, Walmart has taken a broadly collaborative ecosystem approach to fostering change. In the textile industry, for example, the company identified conventional cotton as a sustainability challenge. While Walmart is recognized as one of the best business supply chain managers in the world, when it began to consider textiles, it found it knew very little about the details of the *industry* supply chain. To gain this know-how, Walmart turned to consultants, academics, government agencies like the U.S. Department of Agriculture, and nongovernmental organizations like Organic Exchange and the Organic Trade Association.

Based on the collective wisdom of Walmart's network, the company chose to adopt the Global Organic Textile Standard for its sourcing decisions. It needed suppliers that could deliver on that vision, but this was easier said than done. Cotton producers faced potential risks from converting to organic production: yields fall in the initial years of a transition to organic production before stabilizing and improving; organic markets have also had a history of turbulence. Together, these factors made farmers reluctant to adopt Walmart's standards. To address these concerns, Walmart made five-year quantity commitments to suppliers, and it reduced the number of suppliers it would source from, so that those farmers that got on board would be rewarded with bigger contracts. By helping their partners reduce uncertainty, Walmart shared both the risks and gains of moving toward a more sustainable business model.[5]

The seafood sector presents another example of how Walmart is strategically building an ecosystem of partners to foster its sustainability goals. Wild seafood fisheries have long been in trouble. Annual output has been declining, and some wild fisheries have suffered population collapses. At the same time, demand for wild seafood has been growing at a rate of 25 percent a year. Scientists predict that if this disjunction between supply and demand doesn't change, there will be a generalized collapse of all fisheries in a matter of decades.[6] As a major supplier of seafood, Walmart was in jeopardy. It again assembled a network of experts from different sectors, including historically critical environmental groups. Based on the recommendations, Walmart adopted the certification approach established by the Marine Stewardship Council (MSC), which was developed in 1997 by the World Wildlife Fund and Unilever (a Walmart supplier). Walmart committed to sourcing 100 percent MSC-certified seafood in its stores within five years. In order to provide incentives to fisheries to adopt the approach, Walmart consolidated the number of suppliers to those that demonstrated ability to meet the MSC standard. This in turn ensured expanded and more reliable purchases to companies that could provide MSC-certification.

In seafood, as in cotton and other sectors, Walmart is building an ecosystem of players that provides incentives to break away from unsustainable practices. While many critics have questioned Walmart's motivations, what has been clear is that Walmart's suppliers are working hard to create greener products than they ever have in the past.

A Closing Parable

I close with the story of the giant ground sloths of North America. Unless you're a fan of paleobiology, you've probably never heard it. People tend to focus on evolutionary changes fostered by extra-planetary forces: the potential demise of the dinosaurs in the aftermath of a meteor strike, for example. But most change is caused by the Earth's creatures themselves. Scientists believe the giant ground sloths became extinct around 8000 BC. But they weren't the victims of climate change, habitat destruction, or overhunting. In fact, they not only survived a major change to their environment that killed off similar animals, they thrived. In the end, the giant ground sloths were simply outcompeted by deer and other herbivores that are familiar to us today. The deer used the available resources more efficiently and productively— and eventually filled the ecosystem function so well that the giant ground sloth disappeared. The biosphere creatively destroyed this hapless species.

Conclusion

When you put down this book, you have a choice. One option is to wait for an act of God in your industry to force you to change or for a niche player to prove the value of a more sustainable approach. The other option is to begin proactively implementing the biosphere rules in your organization by building a supportive ecosystem inside and outside your business. I hope my stories of successful innovators have convinced you that applying the biosphere rules isn't a costly sacrifice but an incredible business opportunity. And consider this: if you wait for others to move first, you may become far more familiar with the experience of the giant ground sloth than you'd like.

Notes

Introduction

1. Gregory Unruh, "The Biosphere Rules," *Harvard Business Review*, February 2008, 111–117.

2. Michael E. Porter, *Competitive Advantage* (New York: Free Press, 1985).

3. Robert Ayers and U. Simmonis, *Industrial Metabolism* (Tokyo: UNU Press, 1994); and Robert Ayers and L. W. Ayres, *Industrial Ecology: Toward Closing the Materials Cycle* (Cheltenham, United Kingdom: Edward Elgar, 1996).

4. Dr. James Hagan, Vice President for Environmental Health and Safety, GlaxoSmithKline, personal communication with author, January 24, 2008.

5. Robert Kaplan, "Must CIM Be Justified on Faith Alone?" *Harvard Business Review*, March–April 1986, 100–103.

Chapter 1

1. Tom H. Tietenberg, "Indivisible Toxic Torts: The Economics of Joint and Several Liability," *Land Economics* 65, no. 4 (November 1989): 305–319.

2. http://infochangeindia.org/index2.php?option=com_content&do_pdf=1&id=7161.

3. "Dow Chemical: Liable for Bhopal?" *BusinessWeek,* May 28, 2008, http://www.businessweek.com/magazine/content/08_23/b4087000856552.htm.

4. Lalit Jha, "U.S. Lawmakers Want Dow to Clean Bhopal Gas Leak Plant Site," *Organisation of Asia-Pacific News Agencies*, June 18, 2009.

5. http://skepdic.com/occam.html.

6. R. Brickman, S. Jasanoff, and T. Ilgen, *Controlling Chemicals: The Politics of Regulation in Europe and the United States* (Ithaca, NY: Cornell University Press, 1985).

7. Elizabeth Grossman, *High Tech Trash: Digital Devices, Hidden Toxics, and Human Health* (Island Press: Washington, DC, 2006).

8. http://www.cbo.gov/ftpdoc.cfm?index=4845&type=0.

9. http://ec.europa.eu/environment/liability/pdf/competitiveness_finalrep.pdf.

10. Douglas Fischer, "A Body's Burden: Our Chemical Legacy," *Oakland Tribune,* March 10, 2005.

11. For information, see 3M *PFOS-PFOA Information* portal a solutions. 3m.com/wps/portal/3m.

12. National Center for Environmental Health, *Third National Report on Human Exposure to Environmental Chemicals* (Atlanta, GA: NCEH Pub. No. 05-0570, 2005).

13. Gabe Wing, manager, Design for Environment Team, Herman Miller, personal communication with author.

14. T. Greiner, M. Rossi, B. Thorpe, and B. Kerr, "Healthy Business Strategies for Transforming the Toxic Chemical Economy" (Medford, MA: Clean Production Action, 2006); "H&M's Social Responsibility Report," www.hm.com/corporate/pdf/social.

15. Michael Braungart, personal communication with author.

16. James Ewell, manager, MBDC, personal communication with author, May 20, 2004.

17. Gabe Wing and Scott Charon, managers, Design for Environment Team, Herman Miller, personal communication with author, February 10, 2005.

18. Ibid.

19. See the European Union's REACH Web site: ec.europa.eu/environment/chemicals/reach.

20. Angela Logomasini, "Europe's Global REACH: Costly for the World; Suicidal for Europe" (Brussels: Institut Hayek, November 6, 2005).

21. D. Pearse and P. Koundouri, "Social Cost of Chemicals," World Wildlife Fund, May 2003.

22. Layton, Lindsey, "Chemical Industry Lends Support to Reform," *Washington Post,* August 9, 2009.

23. Michael Braungart, personal communication with author, June 13, 2004.

24. Braungart communication.

25. Gabe Wing, manager, Design for Environment Team, Herman Miller, personal communication with author, April 21, 2004.

26. Ibid.

27. Dr. Michael Realff, personal communication with author, March 13, 2004.

28. http://www.mcdonough.com/writings/promise_nylon.htm.

29. S. Seuring, M. Muller, M. Goldbacj, U. Schneidewind, *Strategy and Organization in Supply Chains* (Heidelberg, Germany/New York: Physica-Verlag, 2003).

30. Ibid., 13.

31. James Hagan, vice president, Corporate Environment, Health and Safety, GlaxoSmithKline, personal communication with author, January 24, 2008.

32. Scott Johnson, vice president, Global Environment and Safety, S. C. Johnson, personal communication with author, April 5, 2006.

33. Miguel Fluxà, Camper, personal communication with author, June 24, 2004.

Chapter 2

1. International Energy Agency, "World Energy Outlook 2007," November 2007.

2. World Energy Council.

Notes

3. International Energy Agency, "World Energy Outlook 2007."

4. Jonathan Rauch, "Electro-Shock Therapy," *The Atlantic*, July/August 2008.

5. "Construction Green Initiatives Flourish Across U.S.," *Engineering News Record—McGraw-Hill*, November 13, 2006.

6. Gronewold, Nathanial, "Green Building: NYC Hails New Eco Landmark, Mulls Sweeping Code Changes," *Greenwire*, July 2, 2009.

7. Thomas L. Friedman, "A Green Dream in Texas," *New York Times*, January 18, 2006.

8. Interviews with Paul Westbrook and Susan Sowell, "Green the New Red, White, and Blue," Discovery Communications, LLC, 2007.

9. Dr. Sultan Ahmed Al Jaber, personal communication with author, June 10, 2009.

10. Gregory Unruh, "The Masdar Initiative," unpublished case study (Glendale, AZ: Thunderbird School of Global Management, 2009).

11. M. Ochsner, C. Chess, and M. Greenberg, "Pollution Prevention at the 3M Corporation," *Waste Management* 15, no. 8 (January 1995): 663–672.

12. K. Nelson, "Finding and Implementing Projects That Reduce Waste," in *Industrial Ecology and Global Change*, R. Socolow, ed. (Cambridge: Cambridge University Press, 1994).

13. Xerox, "The EPA Recognizes Xerox for Environmental Stewardship," *Exchange*, June 30, 2008.

14. "The Wall Street Journal Highlights DuPont's Climate Change Efforts," *DuPont News*, June 9, 2006.

15. "Make Right-Hand Turns to Save Gas," *Money*, http://planetgreen. discovery.com/tech-transport/ups-turns-save-gas.html.

16. Andrew Hoffman, "Molten Metal Technology A," World Resources Institute, 1999.

17. Ibid.

18. L. Johannes, "Molten Metal's Shares Plummet 49% as Agency Declines to Renew Contract," *Wall Street Journal*, October 22, 1996.

19. *Green Panties Hitting U.K. Streets*, http://www.environmentalleader. com/2008/06/02/green-panties-hitting-uk-streets/.

20. DFID, "Energy for the Poor," Department for International Development Report, U.K., 2002.

21. John Elkington and Pamela Hartigan, *The Power of Unreasonable People: How Social Entrepreneurs Create Markets That Change the World* (Boston: Harvard Business Press, 2008).

Chapter 3

1. See L. Goldstein, "The Strategic Management of Environmental Issues: A Case Study of Kodak's Single Use Camera" (MS thesis, MIT Sloan School of Management, 1994).

2. R. Guitini and K. Gaudette, "Remanufacturing: The Next Great Opportunity for Boosting U.S. Productivity," *Business Horizons*, November–December 2003, 41–48.

3. Richard Vietor, "Xerox: Design for the Environment," Case 9-794-022 (Boston: Harvard Business School, 1990).

4. Fuji Xerox Australia Awards at www.fujixerox.com.au/about/awards.

5. Dan Godamunne, general manager, Fuji Xerox's Eco-Manufacturing Centre, personal communication with author, June 13, 2008.

6. Ibid.

7. W. Keer and C. Ryan, "Eco-Efficiency Gains from Remanufacturing: A Case Study of Photocopier Manufacturing at Fuji Xerox Australia," *Journal of Cleaner Production* 9 (2001): 75–81.

8. Ibid., 2.

9. W. Hauser and R. Lund, "The Remanufacturing Industry: Anatomy of a Giant," Boston University, June 2003. Available at http://www.bu.edu/reman/ GetReports.htm.

10. Brian Hindo, "Everything Old Is New Again," *BusinessWeek*, September 25, 2008, 35–40.

11. Godamunne communication.

12. Ibid.

13. http://www.abc.net.au/rn/science/earth/stories/s443426.htm.

14. Godamunne communication.

15. H. S. Heese, K. Cattani, G. Ferrer, W. Gilland, and A. V. Roth, "Competitive Advantage Through Take-back of Used Products," *European Journal of Operational Research* 164 (2005): 143–157; and C. Hawes, M. Rose, and C. D. Phillips, "A National Study of Assisted Living for the Frail Elderly Results of a National Survey of Facilities," Myers Research Institute, 1999.

16. H. Knippenberg, "Océ Asset Recovery," Netherlands, November 2006, http://www.syntens.nl/NR/rdonlyres/E4612CBF-557C-4004-B7C8-F66162063BE4/1914AboutAssetRecovery.pdf.

17. Steve Bradfield, senior vice president for environment, Shaw Industries, personal communication with author, April 20, 2004.

18. Ibid.

19. Ibid.

20. www.shaw.com.

21. Jan H. Schut, "Big German Plant May Relieve U.S. Bottleneck in Recycling Carpet Nylon," *Plastics Technology*, http://www.ptonline.com/articles/200205cu2.html.

22. Scott Vitters, vice president, Coca-Cola Company, personal communication with author, July 24, 2008.

23. Jay Bolus, manager, MBDC, personal communication with author, May 19, 2004.

24. D. Smock, "Design for Disassembly," *Design News*, November 19, 2007.

25. Ibid.

26. M. Toffel, "Strategic Management of Product Recovery," *California Management Review* 46, no. 2 (2004): 120–141.

Chapter 4

1. Kevin Kelley, "New Rules for the Network Economy," http://www.kk.org/ newrules/selected_maxims.php.

2. W. B. Arthur, "Increasing Returns and the New World of Business," *Harvard Business Review*, July–August 1996, 100–109.

3. M. Meyer and A. Lehnard, *The Power of Product Platforms: Building Value and Cost Leadership* (New York: The Free Press, 1997).

4. R. Bremmer, "Cutting-Edge Platforms," *Financial Times Automotive World*, June 1999.

5. Tom Harris, "How Stuff Works: How GM's Hy-wire Works," HowStuff-Works, Inc., http://auto.howstuffworks.com/hy-wire.htm

6. Ibid.

7. Sumi Cate, research and development, Clorox Technical Center, personal communication with author.

8. Bill Morrissey, vice president for sustainability, Clorox, personal communication with author, October 24, 2008.

9. Mark Umscheid, Green Works manager, Clorox Company, personal communication with author, October 24, 2008.

10. Todd Copeland, manager, Patagonia, personal communication with author, July 8, 2008.

11. Gabe Wing, manager, Design for Environment, Herman Miller, personal communication with author.

12. Janine Benyus, *Biomimicry: Innovation Inspired by Nature* (New York: Harper Collins, 1997).

13. "Bezos: How Frugality Drives Innovation," *BusinessWeek*, April 28, 2008, 64.

14. Michael E. Porter and C. Van der Linde, "Green and Competitive: Ending the Stalemate," *Harvard Business Review*, September–October 1995, 120–133.

15. M. Nourreddine, "Recycling of Auto Shredder Residue," *Journal of Hazardous Materials* 139, no. 3 (2007): 481–490.

16. USGS, "Recycled Cell Phones—A Treasure Trove of Valuable Metals," http://pubs.usgs.gov/fs/2006/3097/fs2006-3097.pdf.

17. Phil Levine, "Ford Buys LV Auto Wrecking Yard as Part of Its Recycling Initiative," *Las Vegas Sun*, March 13, 2000.

18. C. Edwards, "HP Gets Tough on Ink Counterfeiters," *BusinessWeek*, May 28, 2008.

19. Sarah Cordero Pinchansky, Biofert, Centro de Investigaciones, INCAE, Alejuela Costa Rica, 1995.

20. Carlos Sanchez, personal communication with author, January 11, 2008.

21. R. Gonzalez, "Raids on Recycling Bins Costly to Bay Area," Weekend Edition, National Public Radio, July 19, 2008.

22. Dan Godamunne, Fuji Xerox, personal communication with author.

23. Ibid.

24. P. Winsemius and U. Guntram, *A Thousand Shades of Green: Sustainable Strategies for Competitive Advantage* (London: UK Earthscan Publishers, 2002).

25. M. Russo and P. Fouts, "A Resource-based Perspective on Corporate Environmental Performance and Profitability," *Academy of Management Journal* 40, no. 3 (1997): 534–559.

26. Jill Dumain, director, Patagonia, personal communication with author, July 8, 2008.

27. Ibid.

28. Todd Copeland, manager, Patagonia, personal communication with author, July 8, 2008.

29. Patagonia, Inc. "Closing the Loop—A Report on Patagonia's Common Threads Garment Recycling Program," The Cleanest Line, March 4 2009, http://www.thecleanestline.com/2009/03/closing-the-loop-a-report-on-patagonias-common-threads-garment-recycling-program.html.

30. http://www.patagonia.com/pdf/en_US/common_threads_pr_expansion.pdf.

31. Scott Vitters, vice president, Coca-Cola Company, personal communication with author, July 24, 2008.

32. Gerry Fishbeck, vice president, URRC, personal communication with author, June 8, 2008.

33. Ibid.

34. Ibid.

35. Ibid.

36. http://www.solsustainability.org/materialspooling.htm.

37. Ibid.

Chapter 5

1. Andrew Orlowski, "Stoic Napster Troubled by Grecian Formula," *Financial News,* July 19, 2006.

2. Gretchen Daily, ed. *Nature's Services: Societal Dependence on Natural Ecosystems* (Washington, DC: Island Press, 1997).

3. Robert Costanza, Ralph d'Arge, Rudolf de Groot, Stephen Farberk, Monica Grasso, Bruce Hannon, Karin Limburg, Shahid Naeem, Robert V. O'Neill, Jose Paruelo, Robert G. Raskin, Paul Suttonkk, and Marjan van den Belt, "The Value of the World's Ecosystem Services and Natural Capital," *Nature* 387 (1997): 253–260.

4. Robert Costanza, personal communication with author.

5. J. Losey and M. Vaughan, "The Economic Value of Ecological Services Provided by Insects," *Bioscience* 56, no. 4 (2006): 311–322.

6. "Buzz Off," *Discover,* October 2009, 38.

7. U. M. A. Partap, T. E. J. Partap, and H. E. Yonghua, "Pollination Failure in Apple Crop and Farmers' Management Strategies in Hengduan Mountains, China," *Acta Hort.* (ISHS) 561: 225–230.

8. L. E. Gregory, M. H. Gaskins, and C. Colberg, "Parthenocarpic Pod Development by Vanilla Planifolia Andrews Induced with Growth-Regulating Chemicals," *Econ. Bot.* 21 (1967): 351–357.

9. Häagen Dazs, "Help the Honey Bees," http://www.helpthehoneybees.com/.

10. http://www.bea.gov/

11. W. Stahel, "Hidden Innovation," *Science & Public Policy* 13, no. 4 (1986): 593–607.

12. Amory B. Lovins, *Soft Energy Paths* (New York: Harper Colophon, 1977).

13. M. Stoughton White and L. Feng, "Servicization: The Quiet Transition to Extended Product Responsibility," report by Tellus Institute, Boston, MA, May 1999.

Notes

14. K. Fishbein, L. McGarry, and P. Dillon, "Leasing: A Step Toward Producer Responsibility," a report by INFORM, Incorporated, 2000.

15. Xerox Corporation, "Environmental Call: What on Earth Are We Doing for Our Customers?," corporate report by Xerox Environmental Health and Safety, 1997.

16. Chemical Strategies Partnership, 2004. Chemical Management Services Industry Report 2004: Executive Summary (San Francisco, CA).

17. Gregory Unruh, unpublished teaching case study.

18. "We Sell Warmth, Not Heaters," The Information Center, Japan For Sustainability, http://www.japanfs.org/db/index.html.

19. Paul Hawken, *The Ecology of Commerce: A Declaration of Sustainability* (New York: HarperBusiness, 1993), 250.

20. Lindsay James, sustainability manager, Interface, personal communication with author, September 5, 2008.

21. Eric Nelson, vice president, Interface, personal communication with author, September 5, 2008.

22. John Bradford, vice president of operations and R&D, personal communication with author, September 5, 2008.

23. Ibid.

24. K. Kelley, *New Rules for the New Economy: 10 Radical Strategies for a Connected World* (New York: Penguin, 1999).

25. http://www.apple.com/pr/library/2005/jun/03recycle.html.

26. Steve Bishop, Brian Walker, Andy Hoffman, John G. Woody, Stuart Rose, Judith Samuelson, Rakesh Khurana, and Nitin Nohria, "Six Critical Conversations About Business and the Environment (HBR Green Conversation Report)," Harvard Business Publishing, September 2008.

Conclusion

1. R. H. MacArthur, "Population Ecology of Some Warblers of Northeastern Coniferous Forests," *Ecology* 39 (1958): 599–619.

2. Thomas Hughes, *Networks of Power: Electrification in Western Society, 1880–1930* (Baltimore: John Hopkins University Press, 1983).

3. Jeff Mendelsohn, personal communication with author.

4. Gunther, Marc, "Wal-Mart to Become Green Empire," *The Big Money/Slate,* July 13, 2009.

5. Erica L. Plambeck and Lyn Denend, "The Greening of Wal-Mart," *Stanford Social Innovation Review*, Spring 2008.

6. Erik Stokstad, "Global Loss of Biodiversity Harming Ocean Bounty," *Science* 14, no. 5800 (November 2006): 745.

Further Reading

The following are some of the many books and articles written on sustainable manufacturing and industrial ecology that serve as the foundation of the ideas presented in this book. The list is too short to give full credit to all those that I have learned from but is a good launching point for those wanting to delve deeper into the ideas and themes of environmentally sustainable business practice.

Business Books

Braungart, Michael, and William McDonough. *Cradle to Cradle: Remaking the Way We Make Things.* New York: North Point Press, 2002.

Hawken, Paul. *The Ecology of Commerce: A Declaration of Sustainability.* New York: Harper Business, 1993.

Hawken, Paul, Amory Lovins, and Hunter Lovins. *Natural Capitalism: The Next Industrial Revolution.* London: Earthscan, 1999.

Industrial Ecology

Ayres, R. U., and U. K. Simonis, eds. *Industrial Metabolism: Restructuring for Sustainable Development.* Tokyo: United Nations University Press, 1994.

Ehrenfeld, J., and N. Gertler. "Industrial Ecology in Practice. The Evolution of Interdependence at Kalundborg." *Journal of Industrial Ecology* 1, no. 1 (1997): 67–79.

Frosch, R. A., and N. E. Gallopoulos. "Strategies for Manufacturing." *Scientific American* 261, no. 3 (1989): 144–152.

Graedel, T. E., and Braden R. Allenby. *Industrial Ecology.* Englewood Cliffs, NJ: Prentice Hall, 1995.

Richards, D. J., B. R. Allenby, and R. A. Frosch. *The Greening of Industrial Ecosystems.* Washington, DC: National Academies Press, 1994.

Nature-Inspired Design

Anastas, P. L., and J. B. Zimmerman. "Through the 12 Principles of Green Engineering." *Environmental Science and Technology,* March 1, 2003, 95–101A.

Benyus, Janine M. *Biomimicry: Innovation Inspired by Nature.* New York: William Morrow, 1997.

Nattrass, B., and M. Altomare. *The Natural Step for Business: Wealth, Ecology and the Evolutionary Corporation.* Gabriola Island, BC: New Society Publishers, 1999.

Robert, Karl-Henrik. *The Natural Step Story: Seeding a Quiet Revolution.* Gabriola Island, BC: New Society Publishers, 2002.

Van der Ryn, Sim, and Stuart Cowan. *Ecological Design.* Washington, DC: Island Press, 1996.

Index

About the Author

GREGORY UNRUH is the director of the Lincoln Center for Ethics in Global Management at Thunderbird, the leading graduate school of global management. An outspoken expert on sustainable business strategy, he is a sought-after speaker and educator, holding positions at Columbia University in New York, Rotterdam School of Management in Holland, IE Business School in Spain, the Fletcher School in Boston, and INCAE in Costa Rica. Dr. Unruh cofounded the Center for Eco-Intelligent Management with the renowned green-designer William McDonough to research cutting-edge sustainable business practice, and shares his insights through public speaking, teaching, and publishing.